Persons a

Theory Redux

Series editor: Laurent de Sutter

Persons and Things
From the Body's Point of View

Roberto Esposito

Translated by Zakiya Hanafi

polity

First published in 2015 by Polity Press

Polity Press
65 Bridge Street
Cambridge CB2 1UR, UK

Polity Press
350 Main Street
Malden, MA 02148, USA

ISBN-13: 978-0-7456-9064-3 (hardback)
ISBN-13: 978-0-7456-9065-0 (paperback)

A catalogue record for this book is available from the British Library.

Library of Congress Cataloging-in-Publication Data

Esposito, Roberto, 1950-
[Persone e le cose. English]
Persons and things : from the body's point of view / Roberto Esposito.
pages cm
ISBN 978-0-7456-9064-3 (hardback) -- ISBN 978-0-7456-9065-0 (pbk.) 1. Individualism.
2. Persons. 3. Property. 4. Materialism. 5. Human body (Philosophy) I. Title.
B824.E8613 2015
110--dc23

Typeset in 12.5 on 15 pt Adobe Garamond by
Servis Filmsetting Ltd, Stockport, Cheshire
Printed and bound in the by Clays Ltd., St Ives PLC

The translation of this work has been funded by SEPS
Segretariato Europeo per le Pubblicazioni Scientifiche
Via Val d'Aposa 7 - 40123 Bologna - Italy
seps@seps.it - www.seps.it

For further information on Polity, visit our website:
politybooks.com

My thanks to Zakiya Hanafi for the linguistic skill, interpretive intelligence, and unparalleled care she has brought to translating this and other books of mine.

Contents

CONTENTS

Introduction

If there is one assumption that seems to have organized human experience from its very beginnings it is that of a division between persons and things. No other principle is so deeply rooted in our perception and in our moral conscience as the conviction that we are not things – because things are the opposite of persons. Yet this idea, which appears almost naturally obvious to us, is actually the outcome of a long disciplining process that ran through ancient and modern history, molding them in its course. When the Roman jurist Gaius, in his *Institutes*, identified persons and things as the two categories that along with actions constitute the subject matter of the law, he did nothing more than give legal value to a criterion that was already widely accepted. Since Roman times, this distinction has been reproduced in all modern codifications, becoming the presupposition that serves as the implicit ground for all other types of thought – for legal but also philosophical, economic, political, and ethical reasoning. A watershed divides the world of life, cutting it into two areas defined by their mutual opposition. You either stand on this side of the divide, with the persons, or on the other side, with the things: there is no segment in between to unite them.

Yet, anthropological studies tell a different story, one set in societies where people and things form part of the same horizon, where they not only interact but actually complement each other. More than mere tools or objects owned as private property, things constitute the filter through which humans, not yet modeled by the dispositif of the person, enter into relationship with each other. Connected in a practice that precedes the segmentation of the social life into the separate languages of religion, economy, and law, these societies view things as animate beings with the capacity to affect their destiny, and therefore deserving of special care. To get a sense of these societies, we can't look at them from the angle of persons or things; we need to examine them instead from the point of view of the body. This is the sentient place where things seem to interact with people, to the point of becoming a sort of symbolic and material extension of them. To get an idea of this, think about what some works of art or objects of technology mean to us today: they seem to be endowed with a life of their own that in some way communicates with ours.

This parallel between ancient societies and contemporary experience is in itself proof of how nothing disappears from history without leaving traces, although becoming reproduced in modes that are often not comparable. It also demonstrates the fact that the modern horizon, genetically composed of the confluence between Greek philosophy, Roman law, and the Christian conception, does not exhaust the arc of possibilities. In the dichotomous model that has long opposed the world of things to the world of persons, during the era of its decline, a crack appears to be showing. The more our technological objects, with the know-how that has made them serviceable, embody a sort of subjective life, the less we can squash them into an exclusively servile function. At the same time, through the use of biotechnologies, people who at one time appeared as individual monads may now house inside themselves elements that come from other bodies and even inorganic materials. The human body has thus become the flow channel and the operator, certainly a delicate one, of a relation that is less and less reducible to a binary logic.

But before tracing out a different way of looking at things and persons from the body's point of view, we must reconstruct the coordinates that for so long compressed and continue to compress human experience into the confines of this exclusionary binary equation. The reason for doing so is because the bodily dimension is exactly what was excluded. This did not take place in the domain of practices, of course, which has always revolved around the body; nor in the domain of power, which is measured by the distinct capacity to control what the body produces. But in the domain of knowledge the body certainly was excluded, especially in legal and philosophical thought, which, generally speaking, has aimed to eliminate its specificity. Because it falls neither under the category of person nor under that of thing, the body has long oscillated between one and the other without finding a permanent place. In the Roman legal conception as well as in the Christian theological one, the person was never coextensive with the living body that embodied it. Similarly, in the ancient and modern philosophical traditions of the West, the thing has been somehow 'decorporealized' by being dissolved into the idea or into the word. In both cases, the division in principle between person and thing is reproduced once again in each of them, separating them from their bodily content.

As regards 'person,' the ancient Greek term from which it originates explains the gap that separates it from the living body: just as a mask never fully adheres to the face that it covers, similarly the legal person does not coincide with the body of the human being to which it refers. In Roman legal doctrine, rather than indicating the human being as such, *persona* refers to the individual's social role, whereas in Christian doctrine the person resides in a spiritual core that is irreducible to the bodily dimension. Strikingly, despite the internal metamorphoses of what we may well define as the 'dispositif of the person,' it never liberates itself from this original fracture. Ancient Roman law was the first to create this rift in the human species – slicing humanity up by thresholds of decreasing personhood that went from the status of *pater* to the reified status of the slave. But the same fracture was created by Christian doctrine in the distinction between body and soul, and by modern philosophy in the difference between thinking substance (*res cogitans*) and extended substance (*res extensa*). In all of these cases, the *bios* is variously sectioned into two areas that are valued differently, one of which is subordinated to the other.

The result is a dialectic between personalization and depersonalization that has at various times been reworked into new forms. In ancient Rome a person was someone who, among other things, owned human beings who were also thrust into the realm of things. This was the case not only for slaves, but also, to varying degrees, for all individuals who were *alieni iuris*, not masters of themselves. In modern philosophy up to Kant and beyond, this relationship of domination was reproduced in the breaking down of subjective identity into two asymmetric kernels, one of which was destined to rule over the other in accordance with its own inflexible judgment. It hardly comes as a surprise in a conception of this sort that the human being is considered to be a composite of rationality and animality, classifiable as a person only to the extent that it is able to dominate the animal that dwells inside it. That the animal within coincides with the bodily sphere, naturally subject to instincts and passions, accounts for its exclusion from the fully human essence. However, what is excluded, because it is extraneous to the binomial equation between person and thing, is the very element that allows for passage from one to another. In effect, how was it possible for entire generations of human beings to reduce other human beings to the status of things, except by making the latter's bodies wholly subservient to their will?

This is just the first vector in the genealogical reconstruction offered in this book. Another vector, opposite and complementary to it, intersects this first one and serves as its counterpoint. To the process of the depersonalization of persons there corresponds that of the derealization of things. The thematic and theoretical epicenter of this book is the bond that ties the two categories of persons and things together, leading them to the same divisive consequences. To understand the significance of this node, we must not lose sight of the paradoxical intersection between unity and division: one serves as the locus where the other is put into effect. Because they are fractured by the same split, despite being contraries, persons and things share a similarity. In the protocols on which our knowledge is founded, things are invested with a separation similar to the one that cuts through persons, such as to cause them to progressively lose their substance. While the law already looked at things from the formal point of view of ownership relations, metaphysics then created a similar effect of stripping away the fleshy part of things by abstracting their material content. The thing was divided from itself as soon as it was rooted in a transcendent idea, as Plato did, or in an immanent foundation, as Aristotle did. In both cases, rather than corresponding to its singular existence, the thing was suspended from an essence that goes beyond it, whether located outside the thing or situated within it. Even Hegel, in a different dialectical horizon, only affirmed the thing as such against the ground of its negative. This implication between 'being' and 'nothingness' [*ente* and *ni-ente* in Italian] that arose as a consequence of the modern reduction of the 'thing' to 'object' is what Heidegger called nihilism.

Language also causes a similar stripping effect when it names the thing. By transforming the thing into a word, language empties it of reality and turns it into a pure sign. Not only does the name of the rose not coincide with the real rose, it also eliminates the singular concreteness of the flower, turning it into a general signifier. There is something more in this divisive outcome than the breach that Foucault saw opening up between words and things at the beginning of the modern era – something that has more to do with the inherently negative form of human language. Language can 'say' the thing only by negating its real presence, transferring it onto an immaterial plane. If we pass, with a wide swing of the compass, from the linguistic sphere to that of economics, we find a process that is not all that different. The reduction of the thing to merchandise, to a consumer product, and then from this to waste material, causes an equally divisive effect. Multiplied by a production that is potentially unlimited, the thing loses its singularity, becoming equivalent to countless others. Once it is lined up in an inventory of interchangeable objects, the thing is ready to be replaced by an identical item, and then, when no longer needed, destroyed. Starting from Walter Benjamin on, even thinkers who view technological reproducibility as liberating the thing from its traditional aura cannot conceal the effect of loss that this reproducibility causes for whoever possesses it.

What I argue in the following pages is that the only way to unravel this metaphysical knot between thing and person is to approach it from the point of view of the body. Because the human body does not coincide with the person or the thing, it opens up a perspective that is external to the fracture that one projects on the other. Earlier I made mention of ancient societies characterized by non-commercial types of exchange. But these – and an irrevocably lost past – are certainly not what this book looks to. We cannot go beyond the modern era, in terms of power or knowledge, by heading backwards. If anything, the parallel that appears is a line of thought that winds through modernity along a different route than the prevailing one connecting Descartes to Kant. The names of Spinoza and Vico and then the solitary one of Nietzsche point to a relationship with the body that is far removed from the

Cartesian dichotomy between *res cogitans* and *res extensa*. It is a relationship that aims to make the body the unique locus where our individual and collective experience are united.

From this perspective, the body not only reconstructs the relationship between persons and things that was shattered by Gaius' great division, it also retraces in reverse the modern passage from *res* to *obiectum* that ultimately hollowed out the thing. The branch of twentieth-century philosophy that reinterprets the relationship between persons and things through the lens of the body is phenomenology, especially French phenomenology. For these thinkers, the human body has a dual function. The first is to fill the gap in the human being between *logos* and *bios* produced by the separating dispositif of the person; and the second is to give the interchangeable object back its character as a singular thing. From this angle, when things are in contact with the body, it is as if they themselves acquired a heart, leading them back to the center of our lives. When we save them from their serial fate and reintroduce them back into their symbolic setting, we realize that they are a part of us no less than we are a part of them. Today, the biological technology of implants and transplants – introducing into the individual body the fragments of other people's bodies or even things in the form of bodily machines – represents a transformation that sweeps over the proprietary boundaries of the person. Contrary to nostalgically reactive perspectives, this anthropotechnology – our capacity to change ourselves – must be seen as a crucial resource, not just a possible risk, for the inherently technological animal that we have always been from our beginnings.

However, given its polyvalent meaning, the human body also takes on a political function that has become absolutely central today. Of course, the political has always had a privileged relationship with the bodies of both individuals and populations. But what up until a certain time passed through a series of categorial filters and forms of institutional mediation has now become a matter directly affected by the new political dynamics. More than a simple backdrop, biological life is increasingly both the subject and object of power. This is the crucial passage that Michel Foucault, before anyone else, called 'biopolitics,' alluding specifically to the prominent role played by the body. Whereas in the modern era the individual was confined to the formal notion of 'subject of law', now it tends to correspond to his or her bodily dimension. In the same way, the entire population has entered into an unprecedented relationship with a corporeality consisting of needs, wants, and desires that involve biological life in all its facets. As a result, the body has increasingly become the issue at stake for competing interests – of an ethical, legal, and theological nature – and thus the epicenter of political conflict. However, this new centrality of the body can lead to differing and even opposing consequences, of an exclusionary or inclusive kind. When crushed into its racial dimension, the body has been the object of an exclusion taken to the extreme of annihilation; in its collective form it can become the agent of political restructuring within a people and among peoples.

Like many fundamental political concepts, the notion of the 'people' bears within itself an inherent duality that tends to separate it from itself. On the one hand, it is the totality of the citizens in a form that coincides with the nation. But on the other hand, starting with the ancient Greek *demos*, the people also designates the part of it that is subaltern, and, strictly speaking, plebeian or 'popular.' Like the dispositif of the person, the people includes an area inside itself that is otherwise excluded and marginalized. One might say that there is a very large part of Western history that rotates around this shifting margin that at the same time joins and separates the 'two' peoples existing in every people. Ever since the ancient metaphor of the 'two bodies of the king,' a disparity – between the head and the body, the king and the people, sovereignty and representation – has always been perceptible in the body politic, one that ensured its functionality. Today, in the contemporary biopolitical regime, this variance is made even more conspicuous by the body's entrance into every significant political dynamic. The person of the leader is no longer separable from the continual display of his or her body, in an overlapping of the public and private dimensions that has never been so utterly complete – like how it inevitably is in today's society of spectacle or how it was in the past in the otherwise different case of totalitarian leaders.

Corresponding to this biopolitical incorporation of the person is the other pole of the political quadrant: the collective and impersonal body composed of masses of women and men who no longer recognize themselves in the representational channels. Of course, the composition of these political subjectivities varies depending on the situations and contexts. But what we see in the resurgence of protest movements that currently fill up the public squares in many parts of the globe is the inevitable spreading of the institutions of democracy beyond its classical and modern confines. There is something in these multitudes, of various types to be sure, that even precedes their demands, something constituted by the concerted pressure of bodies that move in unison. What these bodies signal, with a character that is irreducible to the disembodied profile of the person, is a reunification of the two parts of the people that no longer occurs by excluding one of them. In short, the task that we are called on to perform by these events is to break down the political-theological machine that from time immemorial has unified the world by subordinating its weakest part. To what extent this call will be answered in action remains to be seen. One thing is certain, however: no real change in our current political forms is imaginable without an equally profound alteration of our interpretive notions.

I

Persons

Possession

From time immemorial our civilization has been based on the most clear-cut division between persons and things. Persons are defined primarily by the fact that they are not things, and things by the fact that they are not persons. Between the two there appears to be nothing: neither the sound of words nor the commotion of bodies. The world itself seems to be nothing other than the natural fault across whose line persons acquire, or lose, things. Roman law, starting from Gaius' *Institutions*, established the division between actions, persons, and things as the bedrock for all legal systems.[1] True, this text hardly represents the entire Roman legal conception, but the influence it has exerted on modernity as a whole has been crucial. Few other formulations have exercised an effect of this magnitude for so long. The entire human experience has been cut off by a line that allows for no other possibilities. Every entity the law deals with, if not an action, is either a person or a thing, according to a simple, clear distinction – a thing is a *non*-person and a person is a *non*-thing.

The relation between them is one of instrumental domination, in the sense that the role of things is to serve or at least to belong to persons. Since a thing is what belongs to a person, then whoever possesses things enjoys the status of personhood and can exert his or her mastery over them. Certainly, there are some things that we cannot dominate and that, indeed, in some ways dominate us because they are more powerful than we are, such as the forces of nature – the height of the mountains, the waves of the ocean, and the trembling of the earth. But in general things are considered to be "slaves who never say a word," at the service of persons.[2] They literally take the place of servants. "For if every tool could perform its own work when ordered," Aristotle remarks, quoting a famous verse from the *Iliad* (XVIII, 376) "[. . .] the master-craftsmen would have no need of assistants and masters no need of slaves."[3] We need things. Without them, people would be deprived of everything they need to live, and, ultimately, of life itself. For this reason, the things that we possess are defined as 'goods,' the totality of which constitutes what today we still call 'patrimony' – with reference to *pater*. There's good reason to reflect on the fact that the idea of 'good' coincides with the idea of a thing that we possess: a good is not some positive entity, or even a way of being, but something that we possess.[4] This testifies to the absolute primacy of having over being that has characterized our culture for some time now: a thing is not first and foremost what it *is* but rather what someone *has*. It is a possession to which nobody else can lay claim. Although things were given to human beings in common, they always end up in the holdings of an owner who can have them at his or her disposal, use them, and even destroy them as he or she pleases. They are in the hands of anyone who possesses them.

The latter expression must be understood in its most literal sense. The hand that grasps and holds is one of the distinguishing features of the human species. "With many animals," observes Elias Canetti, "it is the armed mouth itself which does the seizing, instead of hand or claw. Among men the hand which never lets go has become the very emblem of power."[5] When we talk about our hand as the organ that humanizes the world by creating artifacts or sealing promises, there is a tendency to neglect a much more ancient act, that of bare appropriation. The thing belongs first and foremost to whoever grabs it. To be 'on hand' means, prior to being readily available, to be in the grip of whoever possesses it. In order to lay claim to the disputed ownership of a thing, in the Roman forum the litigants physically placed a hand on it before the magistrate. *Conserere manum*, to cross your hands on the disputed thing, was an act closely linked to the physical grasp of it.[6] To complete the ritual of ownership, the individual who claimed to be the owner touched it with a rod (the festuca) while pronouncing the solemn formula "I declare this thing to belong to me . . . in accordance with quiritarian right."[7] The property aspect prevailed even over the identity of the thing. What essentially qualified the thing was not its content, but rather the fact of its being someone's and no one else's, in a form that could not be contested.

This judicial practice hearkens back to an even more ancient ritual, popular in the Lazio region in primitive times, associated with the declaration of war. Livy tells us that the declaration was preceded by a request made to the other people for the return of things held unlawfully. *Res repetere*, to request things, was the last warning before taking them back by force. If they were not handed over, after an invocation to the gods, war was declared (1, 32, 5-14). War itself was always conducted, ultimately, for things – to defend one's own things or to acquire those of others through violence. As Canetti observes, at length "other, more patient means of increase" are rejected and they are thought of as "contemptible. A kind of state religion of war develops, with the speediest possible increase as its aim."[8] For thousands of years, the primary motive for war was looting. Because of this, no traditional commander would have dared to prohibit his men from pillaging. For untold times the capture of things – the mass of booty heaped on the ground at the foot of the winner – stood for power relations between human beings. The land itself was the first thing that the invading army took possession of – by treading on it, conquering it, and enclosing it. Military victory smiled on those who were able, in the end, to take possession of a given territory, on which they planted a flag that was different from the one that fluttered over it before. From that moment on, all the things included in the conquered territory became the spoils of the new owner.

The relationship between war and property long preceded the legally defined one, especially in ancient Rome, the 'homeland' of law: for centuries war was the sole means of acquiring anything unavailable to peoples who lacked other resources. It was the most common way to acquire property – so much so that for a long time piracy was considered more honorable than trade. At its origin, property always refers to a prior appropriation. In its primordial form, property is neither transmitted nor inherited: it is seized. As we might expect, both the transfer of ownership and what would later be called the right of succession were unknown in ancient Roman law. Property had nothing behind it, except the act that made it so.[9] In ancient Rome there was no crime of robbery – partly because the first Roman women were taken in a mythical abduction from neighboring peoples in order to inflict damage on them. In stating that the Romans believed that "whatever was taken from an enemy a man considered to be absolutely his own," Gaius is saying that, when it comes to acquiring things, there is no insurmountable boundary between law and violence.[10] The possible etymological link between *praedium* (landed estate) and *praeda* (plunder, property taken in war) implies the fact that the territorial ground is linked to *praedatio* (depredation, plundering). Not unexpectedly, public acts involving sales and purchases were stamped with the figure of a lance stuck in the ground to represent the strength of the acquired right. Compared to the sharp tip of the lance, the rounded wood of the stick was nothing but a pale symbol. In order for something to become unequivocally one's own, it had to have been torn from nature or from other people. That which is your own, in the strict sense, is what you take with your hand, *manu captum*, according to the solemn institution of *mancipium*. Of course, a legally regulated transfer of property did exist. But the first property was always created by occupying an empty space or by taking possession of an object that had no owner. Whatever had not yet fallen into someone's hands was available to whoever appropriated it. The first owner was identical to the first occupier, just as a wild animal belonged to whoever first sighted it. With respect to this initial act, the role of the *ius* was nothing more than a guarantee. The law protected the owner from anyone who threatened him or disputed his title to the property, reversing the burden of proof onto the disputant.[11]

Roman law is in its essence patrimonialistic. Rudolf von Jhering was right in this sense when he observed that at its foundation there lies the bare economic relationship.[12] Even the state, to the extent that this term can be used to describe ancient Rome, was always thought about in terms of private law. This is why it lacked both a genuine theory of sovereignty and a subjective view of the law – in other words, it is not the legal title that makes someone the owner of a good, but its effective ownership. *Vindicatio in rem*, laying a claim to a thing, consisted in saying *res mea est* (the thing is mine), not *ius mihi est* (it is my right), reflecting the fact that the relationship between the possessor and the thing possessed was an absolute relationship that did not pass via other subjects. Although there were various categories of possession – through purchase, inheritance, and donation – its archetype remained the seizing of a *res nullius*, a thing belonging to no one. In this event, whoever claimed it *pro suo* (for his own) did not invoke any other legal relationship except the ownership of the thing itself. It is as if a part of nature spontaneously offered itself to his grasp, literally falling into his hands. What was no one's now became his; he received it, took it, and enjoyed it. Every other appropriation related to the first one as the original prototype that made all the subsequent ones conceivable. This original appropriation was the irreducible kernel contained in every legal reduction.

The Great Division

Conquered things are subjugated to the individual who claims them as his or her own. However, what is played out in this way is not only the relationship between humans and things, but also that between human beings themselves – their rank, their status, and their power. It is the possession of things, or their loss, that marks the real distinction between winners and losers after a war. Nevertheless, in peacetime, too, possession signals the power relations between various persons and their varying degrees of personhood. The condition of those who possessed a *patrimonium*, like the *patres*, was very different in ancient Rome (although not that different today) compared to those who did not. To possess a patrimony meant not only to have things – including that abstract thing called money, destined to acquire all other things – but also to exert dominion over those who had less, or did not have any at all, and who were therefore forced to place themselves in the hands of the possessors.

This is how ownership of things became associated with ownership over people. Already at this point we see that what was presented as an opposition in reality shows itself to be a mutual implication and, indeed, a dispositif by which persons and things are fitted together in a sort of *chiasmus* structure, a reversed crosswise arrangement, that projects the profile of one onto the other. This is so not only in the sense that relations between persons are defined by the possession of things or lack of possession, but also in the sense that some persons are reduced to the status of things even though they formally remain persons. As Gaius remarks regarding the *summa divisio*, in Rome people were divided into free men and slaves, who thus had a dual status – as persons, to which they belonged on the abstract plane of denominations, and as things, into which they were in actuality assimilated. This ambiguous classification involved not only slaves – placed among the *res corporales* (bodily or material things) and considered to be an *instrumentum vocale* (speaking tool), a thing endowed with a voice, but also other categories like wives, sons, and insolvent debtors who perpetually hovered between the regimes of persons and things. None of these figures had a real form of autonomy – none were legally independent or *sui iuris*.[13] But to be *alieni iuris,* not belonging to oneself, like all those who were not *patres*, meant occupying a domain that was very close to that of the thing.

It is paradoxical that a legal order founded on the frontal opposition between persons and things produced a continuous slippage from one to the other, thrusting some humans into the sphere of inanimate objects. Of course, the reification of the *servus* was not exclusive to ancient Rome. Aristotle had already stated that "a slave is a live article of property. And every assistant is as it were a tool that serves for several tools" (*Pol.* I, 4, 1253b). But this continuous transit between people and things was not simply a functional procedure but the basis of Roman law. If we analyze all the rituals for reducing human beings to slaves, or those for a father to sell a son to another father-master, we recognize this combined personalization and depersonalization dispositif in all its performative effectiveness – as if by way of a sort of proportional inversion, the personalization of some invariably corresponds to the depersonalization of others who are subjugated to them. The more human beings that an individual manages to place on the sloping plane of the thing, the more solidly he or she acquires the title of person. Take the case of the full, unbridled dominion exercised by a creditor on an insolvent debtor, who in the possession of the creditor was reduced to a thing when alive and dead, to the point that even his corpse could be denied to his relatives and left unburied. In this fashion, the amount owing was replaced by the body of the debtor, which became the object of whatever insults or brutality the creditor chose to administer. Never as much as in this case did the interpersonal relationship transmute into a relationship between those who bolstered their personhood and those who precipitated into the infernal sphere of the thing. As Nietzsche observed in this regard, the feeling of personal obligation "had its origin, as we saw, in the oldest and most primitive personal relationship, that between buyer and seller, creditor and debtor: it was here that one person first encountered another person, that one person first *measured himself* against another."[14]

The substitution of the body of the debtor for the unpaid debt gives us a glimpse of an aspect that has until now remained concealed by the binary relationship between persons and things. What relates the two terms to each other is precisely the element that seems to be excluded from the domain of the law, namely, the body. The use and abuse of the body is what leads to the personalization of some and the reification of others. As Simone Weil put it in one of the most pointed criticisms of the notion of person in ancient Rome, "property was defined by the *jus intendi ed abutendi* (the right to use and abuse). And in fact the things which the property owner had the right to use or abuse at will were for the most part human beings."[15] In the regulatory sphere, the living body was granted no legal status of its own, since it was assimilated in principle to the person who embodied it. It could not be the object of negotiation or exploitation – not even by the person who inhabited it, seeing that, according to Ulpian's *Digest* (9.2.13), "no one is to be regarded as the owner of his own limbs (*dominus membrorum suorum nemo videtur*)." In reality, in contrast with this legally protected condition, the body played a prominent role in defining social relations in ancient Rome. It was a work machine, a pleasure tool, and an object of domination. It measured the power exercised by some over others. It was the moving target on which pleasure accumulated and violence was discharged, often at the same time and in a directly proportional manner. Far from being coextensive with the person, as the codes of law would suggest, the body was often the channel through which the person was transformed into a thing. The apparent inevitability of this slippage from one to the other in the very legal system that theorized their absolute diversity leaves one breathless: in ancient Rome nobody stayed a person for their whole life, from birth to death – everybody, for at least some period of time, passed through a condition not far removed from that of a possessed thing.

This variance is an integral part of the category of person since its earliest beginnings. It has been well established that the Greek etymology of the term refers to the theatrical mask placed on the actor's face, but precisely for this reason the *persona* was never identical to the face. The word later referred to the type of character depicted in the play, but this, too, was never the same as the actor who interpreted it from one occasion to the next. The law seems to have reproduced this element of duality or duplicity at the heart of humanity. *Persona* was not the individual as such, but only its legal status, which varied on the basis of its power relationships with others. Not surprisingly, when ancient Romans referred to their role in life, they used the expression *personam habere* (literally, 'to have a person'). *Persona* was not what one *is*, but what one *has*, like a faculty that, precisely for this reason, you could also lose. That is why, unlike what is commonly assumed, the paradigm of person produced not a union but a separation. It separated not only some from others on the basis of particular social roles, but also the individual from its own biological entity. Being something other than the mask that it wore, the individual was always exposed to a possible depersonalization, defined as *capitis diminutio*, which could go as far as the complete loss of personal identity. The category of person, we might say, is what made one part of the human race subject to another, but this was also the case for each and every individual.

As evidence of how long this Roman dispositif persisted, consider the fact that, driven by the goal of re-establishing human rights, even twentieth-century personalism reproduced its core paradigm – namely, the functional separation of the subject from its bodily dimension.[16] As the personalist philosopher Jacques Maritain maintained, the person is "a whole, master of itself" – adding that to be such, that is, a person to all effects, it must have full dominion over its animal part. A human being is a person if, and only if, he or she is the absolute master of the animal that dwells inside.[17] Of course not everybody has the same attitude toward his or her own deanimalization – and the degree of humanity granted to each individual depends on its greater or lesser intensity. This is also the difference in principle, then, between someone who can be defined as a person and someone who cannot, between someone who is in any case a person and someone who is such only under certain conditions. The fracture inside each individual is thus reproduced in the split dividing humankind as a whole. The entire juridical civilization founded on the Roman *ius* bore a clearly visible imprint of this division. As we infer from the celebrated treatise by Joseph Pothier *Des personnes et des choses* (On Persons and Things), in the eighteenth century human beings were separated into classes that were not all that different from the Roman categories, according to a gradation that went from the slave to the noble.[18] For a long time these legal differences were interpreted as genuine anthropological thresholds that marked out varying degrees of humanity. Suffice to say that the institution of slavery, which appears to us today as having faded into the obscurity of a remote past, was only abolished less than two centuries ago – only to reappear, as we well know, in other forms of de facto slavery that are still widespread. The concept of person, which in principle should lead to the universalization of inalienable rights, has long been employed to exclude some types of humans from the benefits granted to others. It has been used to make them into person-things to be used and abused. The only difference between the slavery of ancient Rome, which was later moderated by protective institutions, and that of today is the brutality of the current forms. Between a slave lashed to death in the provinces of the Roman Empire, in the Alabama of the nineteenth century, or today off the coast of Lampedusa, the most appalling event by far is the most recent one.

Two in One

It has been said that the body, precisely because it lacks a particular legal status, is the means of transition from the person to the thing. Not being invested as such by the law, it oscillates between these two dimensions, allowing the transposition of one into the other. This applies to the human race as a whole, cut into segments by anthropological thresholds of separation and exclusion, but also to the individual, who is divided into two areas that are valued differently – one of a rational or spiritual nature, and the other corporeal. This outcome is the performative effect of the dispositif of the person. We have recognized a first matrix for it in Roman law. The second matrix led to the Christian dogma of the

Incarnation of Christ. At first glance, the cultural gulf that separates them might make any juxtaposition seem ill advised. But if we remove our gaze from the historical scenes in the foreground and focus instead on the paradigms underlying them, some surprising homologies come into view. It is the category of the person that makes the points of comparison obvious. How its two conceptions – the Roman-legal concept and the Christian-theological one – became intertwined is a complex question that the literature does not always agree on. Some interpreters point to the influence of the former on the latter, while others reverse the relation. Within the Christian conception, the question is even more convoluted by the way the term 'person' is entangled with the doctrines of the Trinity and the Incarnation. Tertullian made the first attempt to provide an organized framework for the concept, but even in his work there remains a clear discrepancy: in the Trinity the category of person is multiplied by three, but in the Incarnation of Christ it is divided into two.

That being said, and without entering into the complex disputes between the early Christian theologians, which straddle the legal and theological spheres, there does remain a basic symmetry. For both, at the center of the dispositif there lies not only the need to articulate unity and division between them, but the ensuing subordination of one part of human life to the other. These are the reasons I have maintained that Roman law and Christian theology make up the two load-bearing structures of a political-theological machine that was destined to mark the Western conception of power for at least two thousand years.[19] Leaving this question aside, we are still confronted with the central importance that the concept of the person holds in splitting the living organism into two. In Roman law this cleavage affected the entire human species, separating it into areas of different ranks. In Christian theology the same division cut through the identity of the individual, causing a differentiation within it. Unlike what happened in Rome, it is true in principle that Christianity viewed all individuals as persons, made in the image and likeness of their creator. But they are considered as such precisely because they are divided into two natures, one spiritual and the other corporeal, with the latter subordinated to the former. This is how we passed from a functional division between human being and person, as in Roman law, to an ontological division within the human-person composite, between the two substances that form it.

This asymmetric bipolarity between two areas endowed with different values is recognizable, with varying tones and emphases, in all the Christian authors. This is certainly what we find in Augustine, who clearly subordinates the fleshly dimension to the incorporeal one. Although necessary for human existence, the body is nevertheless the lower, degraded part, to the point that the need to overcome the body's needs may well be defined as "a feebleness."[20] Although Augustine changes his tones over the course of his work, the supremacy of the soul over the body is never questioned. This supremacy draws its roots from the insuperable difference that in the person of Christ subordinates the human element to the divine. In line with a typical trait of the political-theological dispositif, what we have in this case is an exclusionary inclusion that is not far off in its effects from the legal version. Once again, the person is the construct through which two realities of a different nature are integrated in a form that subordinates one to the domination of the other. Augustine does not hesitate to establish a sort of formal analogy between the use that God makes of man in the person of Christ and the use that the soul makes of the body in humans (*Letter* 137).

Despite even significant differences, this primacy of the soul over the body was never placed in doubt by any of the classical Christians. Even for Thomas Aquinas, although tempering Augustinian dualism through Aristotle's categories, the person remains the framework within which reason exercises full "dominion over [its] own actions."[21] What in Augustine was only a "use" here takes on the character of a full "dominion." The entire lexicon of the Church Fathers takes shape as a binary configuration that achieves unity only through submission of the lower part. The two cities of Augustine constitute the political-theological archetype from which all other models derive in some way. On a cosmic-historical plane they enact the same conflict that in every person opposes the purposes of the soul to those of the body. Only when we have won the battle against our own body will the city of God prevail over the city of man. History in its entirety is interpreted by Augustine as the battle without truce between the two elements – the human and the divine, the bodily and the spiritual – that in their strife constitute the double-edged unity of the person. Until the war ends, until the powers of the good have subjugated the powers of evil, the conflict will continue in force and the One will remain hostage to the Two.

In Ernst Kantorowicz's great tableau on medieval political theology, two is also the number of bodies that make up the royal person.[22] The founding analogy is the one tying the human body to the dual nature of Christ, transferred onto the exceptional plane of sovereignty. Just as the person of Christ has two substances, one mortal and the other eternal, the king also unites two bodies in a single person – the first transient and the second immortal, transferable to his successors without causing any interruption to dynastic continuity. As far as the workings of the dispositif are concerned, the semantics of the body that are characteristic of Elizabethan England are not significantly different from those of the person, more typical of the continent. In the same way that the person, whether legal or theological, includes a lower part within it, the political body of the king incorporates the human body while preserving its own incommensurable otherness. In this case, too, as in the person, the relationship between the two elements was a disjunctive union. Joined together in the unity of the crown, they diverged at the time of death, when one of the two bodies disappeared and was replaced by a different body. Just as body and soul clashed within each individual, they also collided during life, whenever the king failed in his duties and allowed himself to be dragged down by his instincts. In this event, one body could be pitted against the other – not only by the sovereign, but also by his adversaries. Kantorowicz recalls that during the revolution the Parliament summoned the British people to rally in the name of the body politic of King Charles I in opposition to his body natural, which was subsequently beheaded, without causing any injury to the body politic.

What Elizabethan literature presents in the form of a metaphysical machine intended to perpetuate itself in time can also explode into the tragedy of absolute separation. Shakespeare's *Richard II* depicts the most vivid scenario of this sort.[23] It stages a splitting of the function, which fragments into uncontrollable plurality. The process of decline "from divine kingship to kingship's 'Name,' and from the name to the naked misery of man" is marked by a series of disintegrations.[24] From the triple figure of the King, the Fool, and the God, we proceed to a phase in which the human body begins to prevail over the political body to the point that "kingship itself comes to mean Death, and nothing but Death."[25] It is as if, in its tragic transposition, this splitting of the royal person were to prevail so much over unity that even its memory was dispersed. The split passes through both the body natural and the body politic of the king, cleaving it, with a cross-contamination effect. By the time the king realizes that he identifies not with Christ, but with his traitor, things have gone too far. One body has betrayed the other; Richard has betrayed Richard. The hopeless face of the king that appears to him in the mirror is the emblem of an irremediable bankruptcy. In the scene of the play, the dispositif of the person is shattered into a thousand pieces along with the mirror that reflects it. The two bodies of the king, definitively divided, lie next to one another in the dust along with the broken symbols of kingship. The only thing the king can do is observe that "With my own power my majesty they wound, /

In the King's name the king himself uncrowned./
So does the dust destroy the diamond."[26]

Use and Abuse

While in the Christian conception the dispositif
of the person divides the living being into flesh
and spirit, in modern philosophy it penetrates
into the very consciousness of the individual.
The relationship with a transcendent sphere
is no longer at stake, but that of subjects with
themselves – with the part of themselves that risks
evading their control or even being forgotten. It
was to avert this possibility that John Locke's
Essay Concerning Human Understanding connected personal identity to the workings of the
memory. The memory is the ability on the part of
the I to identify with itself, assuming responsibility for its actions; hence the importance accorded
to the proper noun, as that which strings together
along the same thread the individual moments
making up a life. Who can guarantee that the
old man of today is the young man of yesterday,
or that the madman we see now is the same man
who was once sane? Locke poses these questions
on a purely philosophical ground, but they retain

a number of connections with both the theological and legal aspects of the notion of person. As regards the theological strand, there is some significance in the fact that Locke (partly in dialog with religious debates of the time) refers to the mysteries of the Resurrection, particularly to the possibility that after dying the soul will find itself in a different body from the one it had before. The problem of multiple personalities – two people dwelling in the same body or two bodies represented by the same person – was commonly posed in theological discussions on metempsychosis and the transmigration of souls.

The association of Locke's theory with the law is even stronger, although posited in a form that differs from that of the Roman *ius*. What is missing with respect to the latter is the biunivocal relationship binding the juridical mask to the individual on which it is placed, regardless of the gap separating them. The treatises of the late Middle Ages had already developed the concept of a person that was *ficta* (artificial) or *repraesentata* (represented), referring to an entity that is not necessarily human. Locke dissolves any remaining link with the living body, tying the person to the principle of attribution: in order to define oneself as a person, one needs to be able to prove to oneself and others that one is the author of one's own actions and thoughts. As far as this requirement is concerned, neither the relationship with a given body nor the relationship with the soul is at issue. What counts is to be able to answer for the actions that one has committed, assuming full responsibility for them. From this perspective, the person starts to take on the modern meaning that we are accustomed to giving it – that of an individual who is aware of the consequences of his or her own actions.

However, far from eliminating the splitting, this development ends up reinforcing it. In order for the subject to be able to make a judgment about itself, it must be able to separate from itself, taking on the dual role of the judge and the accused. Indeed, the notion of 'to attribute' is actually connected with that of 'to impute,' both possible translations of the Greek verb *kategorein*. In point of fact, what qualifies Locke's idea of person in its strictest sense is precisely the legal capacity on the part of a court, or even of oneself, to impute to someone the actions that he or she has committed. As we might expect, the philosopher defines person as "a forensic term, appropriating actions and their merits."[27] By making judgment possible, personhood makes condemnation possible. This is how Locke sets up a division in the subject corresponding to the split in ancient Roman law that separated the individual from his or her role and, in Christian doctrine, the soul from the body. By awarding the person the title of "moral agent," Locke simultaneously rendered it the subject of law and the object of judgment – at once justifiable and condemnable. Thus, the philosophical paradigm of the person, aimed at reconstructing the individual identity threatened by dispersion, became the locus of an even more marked division between two planes of consciousness that were destined to never be able to coincide completely.

Kant takes a step further in this direction, establishing in metaphysical terms what Locke distinguished on the basis of function. Not only does Kant cleave the human subject into two different entities, submitting one to the judgment of the other, he also establishes that there is a difference in essence between them. In his *Metaphysics of Morals* Kant places both entities in the regime of the person, but elsewhere he specifies that he is not referring "to a dual personality; only the self that thinks and intuits is the person, whereas the self of the object that is intuited by me is, like other objects outside me, the thing [*Sache*]."[28] It is as if the person expelled one part of itself outside itself, likening it to a simple thing over which it has to regain mastery. In this way, he re-establishes the same mechanism that we uncovered, albeit in other terms, in the Roman legal forum. On the one hand, person is the category that includes both parts, and on the other hand, it is the criterion on the basis of which one of the two poles subordinates the other, making it an entity assimilable to a thing. To use Kant's terms, while the *homo noumenon* is a person to all intents and purposes, the *homo phaenomenon* is such only when he obeys the former. Personality is the ability of the subject to subjugate a divergent portion of itself, along with the willingness of the latter to come under the possession of the former.

What is striking in the author who brought modern thought to its critical apex is the reintroduction of a legal lexicon bearing a clear imprint of Roman law. It is true that Kant reserves the qualification of person only for free men, hence dissolving the contradiction of the *summa divisio personarum*. But then, when it comes to the subordinated individuals, Kant reproduces a relationship of objectification that is not very different from the one laid down in the *ius*, along with several oscillations that actually accentuate the lack of distinction between person and thing. The margin separating them is the quite problematic one that distinguishes ownership from property: "So someone can be his own master (*sui iuris*), but cannot be the owner *of himself* (*sui dominus*) (cannot dispose of himself as he pleases)."[29] What distinguishes the two conditions is the boundary that separates legitimate use from illicit abuse or misuse. The bodies that one has control over but does not own can be made use of but not abused. We should question the crucial role that the notion of 'use' has had in shaping the Western political lexicon. It is difficult to trace out the borderline separating use from abuse, compared to the sharp Roman opposition between *persona* and *res*. Kant blurs the latter distinction by means of a legal category placed precisely at their point of convergence. This is *ius realiter personale*, personal rights of a real kind. Thus, while *ius reale* is a right relating to things and *ius personale* is a right relating to persons, *ius realiter personale* consists in the right "of possession of an external object *as a thing* and use of it *as a person*."[30]

The slippage of person toward thing returns, then, in the author who can least be suspected of an uncritical attitude. In this case, too, the channel of transition between them is the body of the subjugated person, who is thus transferred into the dimension of a possession, a possessed *res*. This applies not only to workers in the service of their boss, but, just as in Roman law, to wives as well – who by means of their bodies can also be appropriated by their husbands as an object of use through the possession of their sexual organs. Kant recognizes that this attribution is inconsistent with the equality for all free people that he himself proclaims. But rather than removing this contradiction, he resolves it by extending the right of reification to the other spouse as well. Thus "while one Person is acquired by the other *as if it were a thing*, the one who is acquired acquires the other in turn; for in this way each reclaims itself and restores its personality."[31] In accordance with the dispositif that directs this entire discourse, personhood is measured by the mutual capacity to use the other human being as a thing. Rather than being the absolute opposite of the person, the thing appears here as the central mechanism inside the category of person – that which, only by having been possessed and consumed, makes the person truly such as the subject of this possession.

This is exactly what Hegel reproaches Kant for in his *Outlines of the Philosophy of Right*, grasping its subalternity to the Roman legal formulation. In spite of the Enlightenment inspiration that fueled his writings, Kant ended up confirming the distinction between persons who are *sui iuris* and persons who are *alieni iuris*, placed at the disposition of the former. This is what Hegel's criticism takes aim at. While Kant does not conceive of the person in universal terms, all human beings must be considered persons regardless of their status. This is what lies behind Hegel's reserve toward the paradigm of person – which he adopts for the legal sphere, but rejects for the wider domain of civil society. However, even though Hegel explicitly distances himself from Roman law, he remains largely influenced by it. When he says that people relate to each other "only as owners," he is suggesting that if the qualification of person is what makes human beings capable of owning things, it is only the ownership of things that makes them persons.[32] Certainly, for Hegel private law is only a partial and inadequate way of experiencing human relations when compared to the higher spheres of society and the state. Rather than complementing the general interest, particular interests tend to oppose it. He takes his criticism so far as to say that "to describe an individual as a 'person' is to use an expression of contempt."[33] This does not take away from the fact that Hegel makes the person's capacity for self-possession the basis for any type of property. Possession of the self is the only kind of possession that is so perfect that it becomes the model for all other types of ownership. But what else does it mean to fully possess one's own person if not to consider it as a thing at the disposition of one's will? As we see, the mechanism that places things at the disposition of persons and puts persons in the regime of things returns once again.

Non-Persons

Hegel's discussion on the person's self-appropriation shifts our inquiry into an orbit that passes closer to us, drawing us into the debate on bioethics in its dual Catholic and liberal versions. As we observed earlier, the Catholic philosopher Jacques Maritain viewed the person as an entity defined by mastery over its animal nature. This particular characterization stems as much from the Christian perspective as it does from the Aristotelian definition of man as a "rational animal," which came by way of Thomas Aquinas. But once this formula is embraced – creating a division in the human species between animality and rationality – there remain open only two avenues, embarked on by the opposing fronts that clashed during the last world war. Either the dimension of reason is crushed into the purely biological dimension of the body, as Nazism did, or the animal part is consigned to the domination of the rational part, as personalism would have it. Thus, unlike Nazism, which by eliminating the profile of the person altogether made the body the property of the state, liberal personalism assigned ownership of the body to the individual inhabiting it. This difference in attribution, which is anything but negligible, does not change the fact that for both the Nazis and the personalists the body is placed in the category of an appropriated thing. From this point of view, because Catholic bioethics deliver the fate of the human body over to its creator, they too remain entangled in a conception that is no different in logical terms from the other two.

As we have seen, if the roots of the Catholic perspective can be recognized in the political theology of the Church Fathers, the dominant perspective of today – that of liberalism – is rooted in a tradition begun by Locke and continued by John Stuart Mill. It is true that Descartes had already declared his belief that "as for the body which by some special right I called 'mine,' my belief that this body, more than any other, belonged to me had some justification."[34] But what for Descartes was still inherent in the sphere of being was shifted over to the sphere of having in Locke's work: "though the Earth, and all inferior Creatures be common to all Men, yet every Man has a *Property* in his own *Person*."[35] By adding that "Over himself, over his own body and mind, the individual is sovereign," Mill simply took this logic to its ultimate consequences.[36] Superimposing the category of property onto that of sovereignty, he made the body into the 'thing' of one's own person. To be grasped in all its magnitude, what Kant writes about *ius realiter personale*, involving the possession of another person as a thing, needs to be traced back to this line of reasoning. Squashed between person and thing, the body is destined to slide from the sphere of persons to that of things. Once this direction is taken, it tends to be followed to the end, just as for Bertrand Lemennicier, when he writes that "Everyone is the owner of himself [. . .]. The human body is an object like any other whose owner is perfectly identified."[37]

But perhaps the most disconcerting aspect of the neo-liberal conception is its explicit resumption of ancient Roman legal categories that goes far beyond even the much more guarded use that Kant made of them. Although Kant in any case presupposed a principle of universalization that was meant to extend the category of person to all individuals, authoritative exponents of liberal bioethics such as H. Tristram Engelhardt and Peter Singer do not hesitate to break this relation: not only is every person not a human being, not every human being is a person. All individuals may belong to the species of *Homo sapiens*, but only some, and only for a limited time, enter into the exclusive territory of the person: "persons in the strict sense, come into being only some time, likely years, after birth, and likely cease to exist sometime before the death of the organism."[38] As in the *ius personarum*, the human race is divided by thresholds of personhood that only fully include adults in good health who are endowed with consciousness and therefore capable of self-determination. Beyond this confine, made mobile by the passage of age and the state of health, there is an expanding list of potential persons (like infants), semi-persons (like the elderly who require assistance), non-persons (such as the terminally ill), and anti-persons (like the insane). The problem, as he insists, is that

> Not all humans are persons in this strict sense, in the sense of being moral agents. [. . .][I]nfants are not persons in this sense. The severely senile and the very severely or profoundly mentally retarded are not persons in this very important and central way.[39]

From here, the idea of 'true' persons having control over the not-yet or no-longer persons follows as a consequence. Since they cannot support themselves, and do not even have full consciousness of their state, they need someone who decides for them – not only about the conditions of their subsistence, but also regarding the opportuneness of keeping them alive or nudging them toward death. We already do this for fetuses. What, asks Singer, prevents the same treatment from being applied to children who are born 'defective'? If we go back to the origin of our civilization, he argues, we can see that membership in the species did not in itself constitute a guarantee of survival. Among the Greeks and Romans, for example, "infants had no automatic right to life. Greeks and Romans killed deformed or weak infants by exposing them to the elements on a hilltop."[40] For his part, Engelhardt, citing Gaius, directly refers to the *mancipium* exercised by *patres* on their children, not unlike the right to prey that places a captured animal in the hands of a hunter:

> Childen, insofar as they remain unemancipated and fail to go out and support themselves on their own, by remaining in their parents' hands are in part owned (or to recall the ancient Roman usage, they remain *in manu* or in parental *potestas*).[41]

Moreover, in addition to the Roman logic, economic considerations now apply that require the number of unproductive human lives to be reduced, in accordance with the principle of proportionality between costs and benefits imposed by the utilitarian model. Accordingly, the good, like pain, is not calculated with respect to individuals but to the community as a whole, which has everything to gain if by renouncing a few lives "not worth living" it may improve those of the others.[42] It is true that there is also a moral constraint toward the members of the species *Homo sapiens*. But only if they are able to fear death and are therefore scared by the idea that they can be eliminated. This is not true for those who are not yet or no longer capable of doing this. Certainly, we must prevent the human beings who are being killed from suffering and ensure that their suffering is no greater than the social benefit afforded by their deaths – but no more than what we do for animals, who possess capacities superior to those of underdeveloped or irreversibly damaged human beings: "whether a being is or is not a member of our species is, in itself, no more morally relevant to the wrongness of killing it than whether it is or is not a member of our race."[43]

It goes without saying that the defense of nonhuman animals is both legitimate and desirable.

But in this case, animal defense is the positive side of a depersonalization that has no precedent in modern philosophy. Singer rightly denies any possible association with Nazi ideology by arguing that the aim of utilitarian personalism is a more just society. But he forgets the fact that no regime has ever proclaimed itself to be acting in the name of injustice, except to identify justice with the biological interests of one segment of humanity. As we were saying, despite obvious differences, it is the overlapping between animal and human implied in the definition of *animal rationale* that links such divergent conceptions to the same disturbing nexus. When reason alone distinguishes humans from their animal part, this can either be elevated to the superiority of personhood or reduced to the inferiority of thingness. What is missing in either case is the acknowledgment of a living body that coincides with neither one nor the other because it is endowed with a peculiar ontological consistency.

2

Things

The Nothing of the Thing

The relationship between philosophy and the thing has always been problematic – not only in the sense that in its singular concreteness the thing is removed from the philosophical *logos*, but also in the less obvious sense that philosophy tends to annihilate the thing. The matter is set out in all its radicalness by Heidegger in his 1949 lecture on "The Thing." In response to the question, "But what is a thing?" he begins by answering in the negative, denying that the thing can ever be considered to be the same as an *object* that is represented or produced.[1] The thing as such cannot be arrived at from the point of view of its objectification. This is the difficulty that all philosophical attempts to think about the thing have come up against, starting from Plato and Aristotle; not to mention scientific language, which, according to Heidegger, led it into an even more blatant deformation. In trying to objectify the thing, scientific language destroyed it before even coming close to it. At this point, concludes Heidegger, "the thing remains obstructed as thing, nullified and in this sense annihilated."[2]

At the origin of this drift, parallel to the depersonalization of the person, there is a semantic change that affects the Latin term *res*, weakening it. This term, which approaches the Greek verb *eiro*, meaning "to speak of something" or "to deal with a certain question," refers to what regards human beings – a case or a cause that concerns them. This is the source of the Italian *cosa* and the French *chose* – but also, in an allied sense, the Old High German noun *Ding*, or *thing*, which refers to a gathering to discuss a controversial issue – an assembly in which something is judged. Its nihilistic outcome, linked more closely to becoming than being, already appears implicit in this juridical aspect that characterizes all the 'names' of the thing, from *res* to *Sache* to *Ding*. The thing, inasmuch as it is 'made' or 'making itself,' is always caught in the legal 'process' that decides its fate in a judging assembly. But even this 'social' significance, so to speak, at a certain point fades away to be replaced by another, more neutral one that refers to an entity that is produced or represented. The roots of the concept-term *ens*, which was widely used in the Middle Ages, run deep into ancient Greek metaphysics, which was also incapable of confronting the thing without emptying it. From then on, what we call 'ontology' was closely intertwined with nihilism, insofar as the semantics of 'being' [*ente* in Italian] were inextricably connected with that of 'nothingness' [*niente* in Italian]. Thus, as soon as the thing was placed in relation to being, it was assailed by the force of negation that the latter conveys.

Why is that the case? Why is it that the thing, when translated into the language of being, is funneled into nothingness? This is the question from which Plato takes his start. Although in the *Republic* he refers to a thing about which "it is impossible to conceive firmly any one of them to be or not to be or both or neither," [3] in the *Sophist* he arrives at an even more disturbing conclusion. Not only is it impossible to deny that nothingness exists, as Parmenides sought to do, we have to admit that being itself is carved out of nothingness. As the Stranger asserts, "not-being was one of the classes of being, permeating all being [. . .]. But now not-being has been found to partake of being."[4] To say what anything is in its individuality, here and now, implies suggesting everything that it is not, or in other words, its difference from every other thing. So, in affirming "this one here" in its uniqueness, the negative penetrates into the positive and takes up residence there as its ineradicable presupposition.

Without venturing too far into questions about Plato's philology, it can be argued that this nihilistic consequence follows specifically from the attempt to save things by attaching them to a transcendent sphere, namely, to their ideal essence.[5] The thing is thus separated, so to speak, from itself and divaricates onto two levels, one of which is external to and overhanging the other. But, in this way, its affirmation on the plane of essences ultimately entails its negation on the plane of the real. Because it can never completely bridge the gap from its own essence, the individual thing is always insufficient and permeated by non-being. From the outset it appears to be lacking with respect to what it nevertheless draws its meaning from. Founded in an idea that is placed on high, but never capable of conforming to it, the thing is left to its own insufficiency. This variance from itself, implicit in the process of 'entification,' is what exposes the thing to the divisive impact of nothingness. By intending the thing as being, the logos ultimately negates it.

Even Aristotle, who also sought to overcome the Platonic 'dualism' between the thing and its idea, remained caught up in the same dispositif of separating and nullifying. Starting from the conviction that "It is impossible for the same attribute at once to belong and not to belong to the same thing and in the same relation,"[6] he ends by arriving at precisely this conclusion. In wanting to close up the fracture opened up by Plato, he introduces the *eidos* into the thing, making the *eidos* its support. The foundation is thus no longer located on high, in the heaven of ideas, but rather below even the thing itself. The *eidos* is the substrate *(hypokeimenon)* of the thing: what remains stable throughout any change. Consequently, the split from the outside world that had been mended now penetrates into the thing itself, dividing it between an underlying, immutable substance and the form that it takes from one time to the next: "From what has been said, then, it is clear that that which comes to be is always composite, and there is one thing which comes to be, and another which comes to be this."[7] In short, since the thing always tends to actualize itself, it is both the same as and different from what it becomes. True, unlike in Plato's schema, this variance does not go beyond the boundaries of the thing. But precisely for this reason, because the split lies within, it cleaves the thing even more deeply. The thing becomes a sort of composite, anything but a cohesive unity, in which what underlies it can never be entirely identical to what emerges on the surface. Form remains separate from matter, just as cause does from effect. Divided between its below and its above, the thing once again threatens to split into layers.

The way to overcome this contradiction is to bind the thing to a principle that governs over its movement. This is what Aristotle defined as the 'unmoved mover,' secularizing the Platonic Demiurge. But this turn in Greek metaphysics only made the heteronomy of the thing even more obvious. The moment the thing was made to depend on an external cause that brought it into being, it had already been conceived as defective and deficient. This paradigm leap went beyond even its (certainly important) theological significance to affect the regime of things itself. The thing now became the product of a craftsman, first divine and then human, on whom its realization depends. This is how all things ended up being plunged into the productive dimension of *techne*. Rather than arising, in accordance with the pre-metaphysical conception, out of the opening of the *physis*, things appear as the result of a creation without which they would not exist. Even without going into detail regarding the decisive role that Christian doctrine played in this paradigm leap, what is evident is the further slide of being toward nothingness that it entailed. When Thomas Aquinas asserted that "All things are, indeed, nothing in comparison with God,"[8] the bond between ontology and nihilism was definitively forged.

The disintegration process of the thing, which went hand in hand with its metaphysical treatment, now seemed inevitable. Its transposition into 'being' anticipated its formulation as 'object,' central to Heidegger's essay on the

"Age of the World Picture." While in the Middle Ages, the thing was understood as *ens creatum*, the fruit of the creative action of God, it was later interpreted as what is represented or produced by human beings. However, by entering into the dispositif of representation or production, the thing – now transformed into object – was dependent on the subject, thus losing all autonomy. As Heidegger notes, this transition appears to be fully accomplished with Descartes: "What is, in its entirety, is now taken in such a way that it first is in being and only is in being, to the extent that it is set up by man, who represents and sets forth."[9] We must not lose sight of the nexus that unifies subjectivism and objectivism while at the same time dividing them: without a subject who represents, there is no represented thing, and vice versa. The ties that the separation between persons and things seeks to sever are once again pulled tightly together. Persons and things face each other in a relationship of mutual interchangeability: to be a subject, modern man must make the object dependent on his own production; but similarly, the object cannot exist outside of the ideational power of the subject. Kant's separation of the thing into phenomenon and noumenon – between the thing as it appears to us and the "thing in itself" – takes this splitting to its extreme conclusion. Never is the implication between the separation of the person and the disintegration of the thing so clearly visible as it is in this case. Each can be divided from the other only starting from what separates it from itself, inverting it into its opposite. Thus, while the person is always vulnerable to becoming a thing, the thing always remains subject to the domination of the person.

Res

Although philosophy tends to annihilate the thing in its conceptual constructs, the divisive effect of the law is no less strong. A long interpretative tradition has accustomed us to juxtaposing the Greek philosophical formulation to the Roman legal experience, along the lines of abstract versus concrete. The abstraction of a world made of ideas, characteristic of ancient Greek metaphysics, is supposedly opposed to the concreteness of the real relations instituted by Roman law. In reality, the relationship between the two worlds is much more complex than this.

Without taking anything away from the paradigmatic irreducibility of the Roman *ius* to the Greek *logos*, there still remain a number of correspondences between them. The law also produces a metaphysics of its own that is certainly different but still related to Greek metaphysics. True, unlike Greek thought, the metaphysics of the law always refers to concrete relations of belonging, transaction, and contract involving the relationship between persons and things. But it does so in a form that makes them abstract, by transporting them onto a general plane. It would seem that in order to act on individual cases, the law has to re-situate them in a world of ideal essences that are animated by a life of their own. For this reason, the 'facts' that the law addresses are not regarded as such, but rather through a transcendental filter that empties them of their concrete content and projects them into a sort of parallel universe. For example, to intervene in a case of buying or selling, the law builds the abstract model of the sale from which it deduces the rules for regulating it. So, just like metaphysics, from which it claims to take its distance, it acts on life by separating life from itself and splitting it into two superimposed planes that are only subsequently reunited. This produces a double effect of emptying and idealization. On the one hand, relations, persons, and things are deprived of any specificity and are related to general formulas; on the other hand, logical structures and ideal schemas take on an ontological status of a phantasmal type that is nevertheless productive of powerful, real effects.

To understand the legal world established in ancient Rome – spreading from there throughout the West – we cannot overlook this peculiar connection between realism and metaphysics, concreteness and abstraction.[10] We have seen the exclusionary effects in the relationship between persons. Something similar occurs with regard to things. The same legal *dispositif* that causes a reification of persons produces a dematerialization of things. Just as people are divided inside themselves by the line that opposes them to things, in the same way things tend to lose their consistency in a formalized dimension that divests them of substance. In Roman law the term *res* does not designate things of the world, even though it remains in contact with these. *Res* has a double status that ranges from an intensely material meaning to a purely formal one. On the one hand, *res* is the thing in its objective reality, and as such it is distinctly different from the person who makes use of it. On the other hand, it refers to the abstract process that assigns it a legal importance. *Res* is what is legally disputed as well as the disputation – thing [*cosa* in Italian] and case [*causa* in Italian] at the same time.

If we lose sight of this distinctive feature – which makes the thing both the object of the procedure and the procedure itself – the Roman conceptual world remains impenetrable to us. To identify its peculiar character, we must avoid superimposing it onto Greek metaphysics or onto the modern perspective, while nevertheless seeking to understand its connections with both. *Res*, in the ancient Roman sense of the term, has very little to do with an element of nature or with a human artifact. It is neither that which has always preceded human beings nor the *obiectum* that stands before the subject – what in German is called *Gegenstand*. As we have seen, in the procedural, legal sense of a "case in question," the term is if anything comparable to the ancient Greek *pragma*, understood as the affair or issue at hand. More than a given, the thing is a *fact* that deeply concerns us, that continuously "calls us into question." For example, *res publica* is what interests us from the point of view of the collective interest, just as *res communis*, by virtue of belonging to no one in particular, belongs to everyone.

When it is said that Roman law is eminently objective, by way of distinguishing it from modern law, which is instead said to be subjective, the term 'objective' should not be understood as relating to material matters. It is true that it is not persons that prevail in Roman law but things, the possession of which makes the persons what they are. Accordingly, things serve to secure the relations between persons, dividing them into different categories, from the *patres* to the *servi*. Precisely for this reason, however, because they serve to establish relations between persons by dividing them into different roles, things maintain a functional status in the legal sense that at the same time empties them of any content. This does not mean that the *res* does not refer to a reality extraneous to the world of nature or to the products of humans; on the contrary, in a horizon that is not theoretical but practical like that of the law, this happens regularly. The Roman *res* is not a purely mental representation, a logical construct with no correspondence in real life. It occupies a space and has a duration. But this does not endow it with a material value. What is of interest to the law about the thing is not the substance, but the formal framework into which it is introduced and that it helps to create. In this sense, in spite of the classical distinction between *res corporales*, which can be touched, and *res incorporales*, which cannot, the things that the law is occupied with all belong to this second category. It is precisely the law, in concerning itself with them, that makes them such. Even those that have a body are virtually separated from it at the time they enter into the sphere of the *ius*. It is as if, in this ghostly universe that ultimately thrusts some people into the regime of things, the material concreteness of things were dissolved and they were exposed to the experience of nothingness.

This consequence follows from the self-referential character with which the law originated, according to an abstract mode that was destined to be conveyed to the modern legal order. From this point of view it could be said that Roman law, perhaps more than Greek metaphysics, constitutes the epistemic model on which the entirety of Western knowledge was formed. But there is another, even more powerful sense in which the negative envelopes the dimension of the legal *res* and comes to characterize it. We are familiar with the strictly patrimonialistic character of Roman law. It considers things before persons and persons always in relation to things. What defines things is their belonging to one or more owners. Even when they do not belong to anyone, in principle they are always appropriable; they never evade the regime of at least potential appropriability. However, Roman law never starts from a positive register of this sort; it always begins from its negative reverse – from the things *not* available for possession.[11] The difference from those that are available is foundational for the law as a whole, to the point of leading off the chain of disjunctions in Gaius' *Institutions*. Things are initially divided between those that are in our property and those that are not. But instead of proceeding from those that are, the legal discourse proceeds from those that are not. Appropriable things are not defined per se, but as the contrary of those that, for various reasons, are not. Very rarely is there talk in the sources of *res in patrimonio* or *in commercio*, except as the negative of *res* that are inalienable, because they are religious or public things. Private law – which in ancient Rome was so predominant as to absorb almost entirely every other legal aspect – presupposes a negativity that calls it into being. This is another trait that runs parallel, although asymmetrically, to both the metaphysical tradition begun by Plato and the Christian conception. Beings are traversed by nothingness because they ultimately issue out of it – from their origin, they are mixed with the nothingness out of which they are created.

Even the legal order preserves a negative foundation: what is lawful is that which is *not* forbidden, just as, in ancient Rome, the people who are free are those who are *not* slaves. The *liber* is distinguished by the fact that he is not *servus*. Indeed, the condition most spoken about in Roman law is precisely that of slavery, which is to say, that of those who have no legal prerogatives. To explain what *sui iuris* means, *alieni iuris* is defined, deriving the meaning of the first term through opposition to the second. This is all the more true for the thing. With a logical procedure that doubles the negation, avoiding the affirmative, *res mancipi* are those which are *not nec mancipi*. The inclusion of something into the sphere of the *ius*, which in Rome ultimately comprises all things, always arises out of an exclusion. What is excluded is not that which is not included; rather, what is included is that which is not excluded. When examined closely, all the distinctions that stem from each other in an unbroken chain of alternatives, starting from the *summa division*, conform to this negative register. No category is ever defined in itself, but through what diverges from it. Just as appropriable things are *other than* appropriable ones, *res humani iuris* are those that are *non divini juris*. In the context of human law, in their turn, private things are those that are *not* public. And even among public things, those that belong to the state are those that do *not* belong to everyone, defined instead as *communes*. However, belonging to everyone – a further and final divergence – is not the same as *nullius*, belonging to no one, because while the former remain in any case inappropriable, the latter, although unappropriated for the time being, are nevertheless appropriable by whoever first lays hold of them. Thus, the included is generated out of what is excluded, and the positive out of the negative.

Words and Things

Even before the Roman *ius* and the Greek *logos*, the experience of language was already there to negate things in their living content. This contrasts with the widespread idea that language is a simple vehicle of expression, and that there exists a natural, or even artificial, correspondence between words and things – words as the verbal form of things, and things as the content of words. Certainly, as recounted in Genesis, when language was given to humans by God, it was the sign itself of things: language resembled things so closely that it revealed them with utter transparency. Meaning thus seemed to spring forth from things like a source from a rock or light from the sun. Later, with the collapse of the tower of Babel, that correspondence was broken. While languages continued to multiply, an ever wider gap opened up between things and each of the vernaculars. In the fifteenth century, language still seemed to be part of the world, but already by the end of Renaissance Humanism, language had withdrawn from the world, closing itself up in the abstract space of representational signs. The ancient bond between words and things had now been broken. The name of things inscribed on their skin began to fade, while words lost any direct access to the life of things. Not only was language now no longer capable of revealing the enigma hidden inside things, it actually tended to make it more and more indecipherable. Don Quixote's hallucinatory experience in the autumn of the Renaissance marks the end of similitude between being and its signs: "The written word and things no longer resemble one another. And between them, Don Quixote wanders off on his own."[12] By now distant from things, words take refuge in the folds of books or get all jumbled up in the depths of madness. Since language is no longer a picture of the world, it can at most attempt to translate what it was naturally incapable of expressing. For Descartes, truth no longer resides in the nexus between words and things, but in the evident perception of a consciousness present to itself. No longer is there anything that can guarantee some sort of correspondence between signifier and signified. In the new regime of meaning, the profile of difference replaces the face of similarity, disfiguring it. For representation to exist, there must be a distance between sign and signified. In order to state the thing, language must be detached from the thing and isolate itself in its own self-referential universe.

But if so, every statement ends up having a negative impact. Language can affirm the thing only by denying its living presence. What Foucault views as the opening of a breach may well be understood as a work of negation. Rather than attributing the break to the advent of a new episteme, it can be explained by the structure of the linguistic act. The naming of things on the part of language is anything but a neutral act: rather, it has the character of a violent intrusion. It would seem that in order for language to appropriate things, which are now separate from it, it has to project the fracture that it bears within itself into things. In any case, the idea that language is characterized essentially by negation is a fact not always picked up on by philosophers, but very much present to linguists. For Ferdinand Saussure, "language rests on oppositions, on a network of wholly negative values which exist only in mutual contrast."[13] It is distinguished from prelinguistic communicative codes, which are naturally oriented toward agreement, by its capacity to negate what it represents. The use of 'not,' as it has been observed, is the most significant prerogative of human discourse.[14] But, on closer examination, the negativity of language, as well as the act of representing, also affects the reality of what it represents. What is negated in the linguistic procedure is not only a given mode of being of the thing, but, in a sense, its very existence. To name the thing, language must transpose it into a dimension different from the real one. Not having any constitutive relationship with the things that they name, in short, words take away the reality from them that they nevertheless seek to express about things. Only by losing their concrete existence are beings linguistically representable. The very moment the thing is named, it loses its content and is transferred into the insubstantial space of the sign. In this way, its possession by language coincides with its annihilation.

This nihilistic dispositif is central to Hegel's philosophy. Although in the first pages of *The Science of Logic* he brings into awareness the relationship between being and nothingness already discerned in Plato's *Sophist*, in the *Phenomenology of Spirit* he attributed it to the divisive power of language. The singular thing – this piece of paper, this tin box, this glowing spark – is unattainable by a language designed to express itself according to universal concepts. He writes:

> In the very attempt to say it, [the thing] would, therefore crumble in their hands; those who have begun to describe it would not be able to finish doing so: they would have to hand it over to others, who would themselves in the last resort have to confess to speaking about a thing that has no being.[15]

The instant language tries to grasp the 'this' – which is to say, the thing in its singular concreteness – language negates it by transferring it onto the abstract plane of categories. This happens because, to grasp something conceptually, we must recognize the negative that constitutes it dialectically. Language can express what it is only by presupposing its negation. The naming of things, the instant they are assigned to the class that includes them, wipes out their empirical being, reducing them to an infinite series. To represent things in their essence, language abolishes them in their existence. In brief, the word conveys being to us, but separated from its singularity and reduced to abstraction.

This negative power of language is not, as Foucault viewed it, the result of a fracture in the order of discourse that was reached at a certain point, but an original given, traceable to its genesis: "Adam gave a name to all things. This is the sovereign right, its primal taking-possession of all nature."[16] Commenting on this famous passage from Hegel, Maurice Blanchot went so far as to say that language, as the preface to each word, requires "a kind of immense hecatomb, a prior deluge, plunging all of creation into the sea."[17] After humans had annihilated all beings, simply by speaking, God had to recreate them from scratch from the nothingness out of which they slid. This is how a being made of nothing took the place of the individual beings that were fixed in their concrete existence. Of course, language does not physically kill anyone. But when someone says 'this cat' or 'this woman,' they are taken out of their immediate presence and consigned to absence. Blanchot infers from this that language establishes a relationship between things and death, so that "it is accurate to say that when I speak, death speaks in me."[18] From this perspective, the fate of things comes to approach more closely that of persons. Although divided by an unbreakable limit – or rather, precisely because of this – it is as if the power of nothingness was communicated from one to the other. The death that language confers on things bounces back, returning to the subjects who make use of it. The power to speak is allied to a void of substance that is communicated by the words of those who utter them, dragging the speaker into the same vortex: "When I speak, I deny the existence of what I am saying, but I also deny the existence of the person who is saying it."[19]

The only type of language that "saves" the thing is literary language. And this is not because it preserves things in their being, but because it takes for granted that by giving things meaning, it destroys them. The ideal of literature, as Blanchot recalls it, is to say nothing; or to say nothing at all, knowing that the written word owes its meaning to that which does not exist. Unless, that is, one understands words themselves as the places in which they are deposited – a sheet of paper, a shard of rock, the bark of a tree – as things, the only ones that remain alive. While common language leaves things separated from words, in literary language words are made into new things that live off the nothingness introduced into them. Literature takes things at their origin and at their final fate. It does not attempt, in vain, to remove them from nothingness. It accompanies them in their drift. On the one hand, literature is this great force of destruction – the most violent devastation of the natural character of things. On the other, it is the form of supreme attention to what remains of things, to the ashes left behind by the fire. Literature

> is not beyond the world, but neither is it the world itself: it is the presence of things before the world exists, their perseverance after the world has disappeared, the stubbornness of what remains when everything vanishes and the dumbfoundedness of what appears when nothing exists.[20]

The Value of Things

In the modern world things are annihilated by their own value. This formulation only comes as a surprise if we attach an ethical connotation to the term 'value,' which, under the process of secularization, has been emptied of meaning by being transposed into an economic dimension. The worth of a thing is determined by objective parameters that have little to do with its intrinsic quality. This general process of exploitation, which affects modern society as a whole, is reconstructed in each of its steps by Karl Marx. Commodities, to which things have been largely reduced, have a use value relating to the way they are used, and an exchange value, defined instead by the time required to produce them. This second type of value, which can be expressed in a single unit of measurement, allows goods to be exchanged in the market. When considered in terms of their use value, things preserve their peculiar quality, but when treated according to their exchange value, they lose it. This is why, instead of strengthening their meaning, the value of things flattens them into a undifferentiated series. However, Marx brings to light a further and even more powerful effect of derealization. As he wrote in a famous passage on the fetishism of commodities, when a table is used as such it remains the wooden object that we all know, but as soon as it is put on the market "it is changed into something transcendent. It not only stands with its feet on the ground, but, in relation to all other commodities, it stands on its head."[21] What causes this phenomenon of inversion, which shares many features with a magic spell, is precisely the exchange value that makes each product of labor a sort of "social hieroglyphic."[22] What people perceive as the natural qualities of things are in reality the social relations congealed in them: "it is a definite social relation between men, that assumes, in their eyes, the fantastic form of a relation between things."[23]

Here, in this classical chiasmatic interpretation, there reappears the link between persons and things with which we started. Their division not only appears as a form of implication, but as a true metaphysical exchange that transmutes the ones into the others. What appear to be things are nothing but the reversed outcome of relationships between people. Money, having become capital, constitutes their eminent expression – as pure exchange value, it is regarded as the most valuable thing to possess. But in addition to this first spell, which attributes to things the autonomy of figures endowed with their own life, there comes an inverse, complementary enchantment that turns people into things. Marx's analyses of reification are well known and commented on by a large literature. In the capitalist market an entire class of people becomes a product that is freely purchasable and exchangeable on the market. Like any other commodities, labor-power also has an exchange value, which is proportional to the time necessary for its production. The latter exercises full domination over those who believe it to be at their disposition. In short, while transforming things into commodities, people transform themselves into things. This applies in the first place to those who are chained to the mechanism of production as modern slaves. But, in general, it applies to everyone. Even the capitalist is locked into the dispositif of exploitation in a self-sustaining fashion. He is occupied with maximizing the value of value in the same way that he reproduces production. These are the two sides of a mechanism that, while it personifies things, 'thingifies' people to an extent unknown in previous societies. In these societies "the social relations between individuals in the performance of their labour, appear at all events as their own mutual personal relations, and are not disguised under the shape of social relations between the products of labour."[24] In the capitalistic regime, the opposite occurs. In the same way that workers are "personified labour-time,"[25] similarly, the capitalists become "capital personified," "personifications of capital and wage-labour."[26]

This process, grasped by Marx in terms of a critique of political economy, lends itself naturally to other interpretations. During the 1920s, while Georg Lukacs was emphasizing its reifying aspect, Walter Benjamin, in a more dynamic perspective, recognized its power to transform ancient orders. The fact that alienation affects the nature of the thing, in addition to the work required to produce it, is a premise that requires demonstrating. By positing the 'good' of things as outside them – by separating their nature from their value – Marx evinces a distant Platonic influence. From this, too, comes his pathological concept of "fetishism," later picked up on by Sigmund Freud. This is exactly what Benjamin counters in his essay on "The Work of Art in the Age of Mechanical Reproduction." Going against the anti-technological trend that permeated the entire culture of the time, what he identifies in the unlimited repeatability of the work of art is something that profoundly transforms the aesthetic perception. The destruction of the "aura" frees the object from the Romantic sheath that envelopes it, infinitely prolonging its life. Whatever is endlessly reproducible is, in principle, eternal. But this is an inherently contradictory process, given that the extension in time is paid for by a diminished ontological depth. It is almost as if the thing, by projecting itself into the future, loses its rootedness in the past and, along with it, the capacity to bear witness to the present:

> The authenticity of a thing is the essence of all that is transmissible from its beginning, ranging from its substantive duration to its testimony to the history which it has experienced. Since the historical testimony rests on the authenticity, the former, too, is jeopardized by reproduction when substantive duration ceases to matter.[27]

It might well be said that both aspects Benjamin perceived have been reflected in our contemporary world. On the one hand, as anthropologists of art point out, artistic objects experience a subjectivity that makes them more akin to personal beings endowed with their own capacity to act than to simple things.[28] This is what prompted Günther Anders to speak of a psychology of things.[29] Technology, in a form no different from art, can also confer a sort of life of relation to objects, especially to electronic or telematic ones. Unlike the work of art, however, this seems to arise from their internal mechanism, independently of whoever activates it. This autonomy, which seems to lend a personal profile to things, is precisely what produces an effect of depersonalization in those who, no longer being subjects, become passive objects. This is the line of reasoning behind Simone Weil's observation that "As collective thought cannot exist as thought, it passes into things (signs, machines . . .). Hence the paradox: It is the thing which thinks, and the man is reduced to the state of a thing."[30]

Here we have the other perspective from which the problem can be examined. The process of personalizing things now appears in an inverted mirror image, as the outcome of the reification of persons. At the source of this interpretative strand, not necessarily opposed to the first, there stands Heidegger. In a lecture given together with the one on "The Thing," he begins by saying that as much as its lost fragments may be precious to us, each thing acquires the characteristics of its equivalent. With respect to the modern transformation of the thing into an object, there is a further step that makes the object a simple "standing reserve [*Bestand*]." With its advent, even what remained present of the being disappears. The resource is positioned not in itself, but in view of its use. Thus the coal that is used to fuel a power plant is not a thing in the same way as the jug on the table. While the jug does not produce anything other than its simple presence, coal is brought into being to generate heat. Here, as in Marx, production and exploitation converge in the same effect of derealizing the thing; with the difference that, rather than attributing this outcome to the thirst for profit, Heidegger connects it to the tendency to use everything that is at our disposition – this is also the literal meaning of the term "dispositif." What is at our disposition is always also replaceable with something equivalent and therefore, in the final analysis, superfluous. Unlike Benjamin, in short, Heidegger sees in the reproducibility of the thing not its possible extension, but its potential elimination in favor of another thing that is fully equivalent. In positionality [*Gestell*], "the one drives the other ahead."[31]

Each piece into which the thing is shattered is in this sense a 'spare part,' replaceable by another equivalent one. This means that the more the thing is reproduced, the less it exists as such, other than as "something to lose" or waste material. But Heidegger adds another consideration that once again concerns the antinomic link between thing and person. The fate of one is refracted by that of the other. The subordination of the thing to the cycle of reproduction is no different, in essence, from that of human beings themselves, who, while believing that they govern it, are actually governed by it. Humans are also in their own fashion "pieces of the standing reserve," always replaceable by another. Certainly, they belong to the machinery in a different way from machines, but they remain caught in its gears, whether they have contributed to building it or simply make use of it. Even when one is distant from it, as in the case of a forester who goes along the same path taken by his forefathers: he too, whether he knows it or not, is sucked into the same mechanism in which the reserves of cellulose stock for newspapers and magazines end up. Or as it happens to "every radio listener who turns its dial, [he] is isolated in the piece character of the pieces of the standing reserve, in which he remains confined even if he still thinks he is entirely free to turn the device on and off."[32] Just when the person imagines he has attained full control over the thing, now reduced to an infinitely reproducible and replaceable piece, he enters unwittingly into the same condition as the thing.

Das Ding

It may seem paradoxical to state that the thing is threatened by an excess of reality. It has been observed, by various thinkers, that after the unrealistic delirium of the postmodern period, the pendulum of thought is now shifting toward a new realism.[33] Although with a different intention, Alain Badiou previously argued that the last century was characterized by a passion for the real.[34] Long entangled in a symbolic net, the thing itself in its absolute nakedness is now coming into view. But what is the effect of our encounter with it? What does a thing that has been denuded, deprived of symbolic resonances, clinging to itself all the way to the edge, have to say to us?

First of all, it behooves us to ask ourselves whether, and to what extent, this pressing demand for reality contrasts with the nihilism that preceded it. For Jean Baudrillard, for example, contemporary hyperrealism is the continuation and counter effect of an identical process of derealization. At its origin there lies the transfer of the thing that we discussed earlier from the natural phase of use value to the commercial one of exchange value. But after this first mutation, analyzed in its reifying consequences by Marx, there followed a second, even more drastic one that sucked the thing into the phantasmal world of the simulacrum.[35] With it disappeared any association with an objective referent. Once universal equivalence was achieved, signs were exchanged among themselves without reference to anything else. There was no more need to signify something. With the disappearance of the finality of actions, opposites ended up overlapping. Marx's dialectic between use value and exchange value, like the one between forces of production and relations of production, was neutralized by a general lack of differentiation. Even money, which up to a certain point was still bound to the gold standard, has entered into the arena of financial speculation and refers to nothing outside its own unlimited circulation. It is as if each thing was doubled in a copy so identical to the original that the copy merged with the original. In the infinite series in which objects multiply, they become a simulacrum of each other and, therefore, of themselves.

However, the doubling of the thing in its simulacrum displays a character that is in itself ambivalent, expressing both intensification and emptying. Emptied of symbolic effectiveness, the thing is folded back on itself and duplicated. While realism still refers to an objective referent, and surrealism submits the real to the test of the imagination, hyperrealism eliminates even the latter distinction, making one the expression of the other. The outcome is a sort of hallucination that makes each thing a copy of its own copy. The real, in this case, is what gives rise to a perfect reproduction. It is reality passed through the sieve of reality, deprived of all reflection, closed in on itself: "Yet things continue to function long after their ideas have disappeared, and they do so in total indifference to their own content."[36] There is something in this desymbolization of things that corresponds from the other side of the mirror to the reifying fate of persons. Separated from them, things split even within themselves: "A thing which has lost its idea is like the man who has lost his shadow, and it must either fall under the sway of madness or perish."[37] This is the consequence of a negative saturation – an excess extenuation. In a sort of infinite excrescence, in which gestures and events accumulate for no reason, things are annihilated by their own proliferation.

In the "integral reality," which coincides down to the last detail with the virtual one, truth and appearance are superimposed in a perfect correspondence. Flattened into their content, devoid of any reference to other things, things chase after each other on a surface that has no depth:

> Once all transcendence is conjured away, things are no longer anything but what they are and, such as they are, they are unbearable. All illusion is gone from them and they have become immediately and totally real, with no shadow and no commentary.[38]

Having reached its critical mass, reality runs the risk of self-destructing. From this point of view, one might well say that it is the excess of real, its hyperreal intensification, that is exactly what removes the world from the reality principle. It is as if, in the void of meaning, every metaphor became real, thereby losing itself as such. What remains in the hallucinatory correspondence between signifier and signified is a mute reality, removed from communication, locked up in its own confines.

This is how Lacan defines the Thing – *das Ding*, differentiating it from *die Sache*. Although both terms refer to legal proceedings, to judicial practice or to the debate that introduces it, they differ greatly in their meaning. While *die Sache* is the product of human action that can always be spoken and related to a case [*causa* in Italian] to which it remains essentially tied, "*das Ding* is found somewhere else."[39] On several occasions Lacan insists on its absolute heterogeneity. Introduced by Freud especially in his essay on negation, *das Ding* refers to an irreducible alterity: "There is something different in *das Ding*."[40] It is as if Lacan hesitated to speak about it, locating it in an area to which the word has no access: "What one finds in *das Ding* is the true secret."[41] By this, he does not mean to say that it is unreachable because of its remoteness. On the contrary, it is what lies closest to us – or, better, what lies within us and dwells inside us, but as something completely foreign. In *das Ding*, proximity and distance, identity and cleavage, intimacy and alienation overlap – where the concept of 'alien' must be allied with that of 'hostile,' as that which threatens us from inside. Although fully internal to the subject, *das Ding* is its absolute Other.

While Freud places it beyond the pleasure principle, where the life force intertwines with the death drive, Lacan inscribes it in the sphere of enjoyment, or *jouissance*, which is different from and opposite to that of desire: "for desire comes from the Other, and *jouissance* is located on the side of the Thing."[42] This is another, much more disturbing way of looking at the passion of the real that haunted the century. From this perspective, the Thing appears to us in all its threatening presence. With the membrane that makes it unattainable to desire now torn, the imperative of *jouissance* brings us closer to the heart of the Thing, to its glowing core. No longer covered by protective barriers that shelter us from its searing rays, it appears to us in nauseating and violent proximity. When the veil that covers it – the symbolic network that aggregates human experience in the connection of social relationships – is torn away, the terrifying aspect of the Real is revealed. It is all that remains of reality once it is deprived of its phantasmal support. When this happens, no longer barred as it was in the infinite deferment of desire, the Thing becomes directly present to us. This de-sublimation of the object causes a collapse of the symbolic space, promoting an immediate relationship with the Other. Trying, in vain, to appropriate the thing, we become caught in a form that both terrorizes and disgusts us.[43]

Slavoj Žižek recalls the final scene of the film *Matrix*, in which the protagonist, who has returned to the landscape devastated by planetary war, is accepted by the head of the resistance, Morpheus, with the ironic comment "Welcome to the desert of the real."[44] Stripped of any further meaning, crushed into its own immanence, the real shows us its deadly face. It always remains one step beyond what we are able to bear (like Pier Paolo Pasolini's 'unbearable' film, *Sade*). Between what is only real – which is to say, socially mediated – and the Real, understood in its excessive aspect, there is the same distance that separates a simple tattoo from the wounds that cutters inflict on themselves, or what is referred to as snuff porn, in which the actors undergo real torture, from normal erotic movies. In this going beyond, there is both a fulfillment and a reversal of meaning. When reality is integral, doubling itself in hyperreality, it reveals a glimpse of its virtual, highly spectacular face.

The explosion of the Twin Towers, often interpreted as the return of the real into a world of illusions, brought back these two inextricably intertwined aspects. With its unprecedented violence, this tragic event can be seen as the Real pushed beyond itself. Replicated countless times on television screens, the scene can be viewed as what leads us into the "desert of the real" and, at the same time, as a television production – the latest and most impressive of Hollywood films. At the beginning of the new century, the reversibility thus became complete: just as the postmodern trend reversed itself at a certain point into a new realism, the latter now acquired new 'special effects.' The moment the virtual rigidified into the real, the real itself became virtual. The reason some viewed the attack on the Twin Towers as a culmination of contemporary art is not that hard to understand: it was a spectacular event that surpassed both reality and appearance in their indiscernible indistinguishability. Most probably, it is our inability to withstand the direct encounter with the Thing that transmutes it into a nightmare – a horrifying mixture of dream and reality. What is defined as the "return of the real" conceals within itself this annihilating maelstrom. The thing is snatched away from us by the same movement that draws it near to us.

3

Bodies

The Status of the Body

It may appear odd that the human body was
excluded from the horizon of the law for such
a long time. Perpetually disputed by the various powers that claimed ownership over it – the
state, the Church, the individual – the body
never benefited from an adequate legal definition.
Introduced into early English writs at the dawn
of modernity, through the *habeas corpus* formula,
the body then disappeared from European civil
codifications, which were constructed around
the abstract framework of disembodied subjects.
Mentioned only in connection to the first and
last moments of birth and death, the body was

viewed as a natural given that apparently required no special legal attention. This exclusion was the inevitable consequence of the great division that organized our way of thinking. Because the human body does not fall naturally under the category of person or thing, it was omitted as an object of the law and left to vacillate between one and the other. In actuality, in line with the Roman tradition, the prevailing trend until a few decades ago was to assimilate it to the concept of person. On the basis of Ulpian's well-known formulation, according to which the body of a free man can never be assigned an economic value, any approximation with the thing has always been avoided. Consequently, since there are no intermediate stations between thing and person, the only choice has been to locate the body in the orbit of the person. Despite noting all the attendant contradictions, it was Kant who came to the clearest conclusion:

> Man cannot dispose over himself, because he is not a thing. He is not his own property – that would be a contradiction; for so far as he is a person, he is a subject, who can have ownership of other things.[1]

This proposition serves as the basis for Article 1128 of the French *Code civil*, which excludes the body from things exchanged in commerce. It also serves as the basis of the European Union's Charter of Fundamental Rights (3.2), which prohibits "making the human body and its parts as such a source of financial gain."[2]

But paradoxically, precisely by declaring the body to be a 'person,' such prohibitions have had the unintended effect of sending it back to the status of *res*, albeit *extra commercium* (out of commerce). In actuality, maintaining that something is not an object of commerce is not equivalent to excluding it from the regime of things. An even greater difficulty emerges when the body is situated in time and space rather than being considered in the abstract. In terms of time, it is commonly held that "death forces the body into the category of things."[3] In this regard, Pierre Legendre recalls the case of Saint Spiridon, the fourth-century bishop of Cyprus. The saint's mummified corpse was brought to Corfu by a Cypriot family fleeing from the Turks, as part of its private estate, eventually becoming a dowry for the daughters. What the human body is before birth, when it is still an embryo, gives rise to a similar ambiguity. At what point can it start being considered a person? When does it stop being considered one, and become a thing? Should the stealing of a corpse or an embryo be regarded as kidnapping, as if it involved a person, or should it be treated as theft, as if it involved a thing?

The question is posed in an even more unanswerable fashion when the body is considered in terms of its individual parts – its products or separate organs – rather than as a whole.[4] In general, once a part is removed from the body, it is treated as a thing. However, this choice does not come without adverse effects, at least as regards certain organs. The question does not arise for teeth, nails, or hair once they have been extracted or cut, because they are easily construed as falling under the condition of *res nullius*. However, the case of blood, because of its symbolic importance, is more complex. Although not considered reducible to a thing, blood is often commercialized for the purpose of blood transfusions. There has been even more marked legal indecision in the case of a gallbladder extracted from a patient and used for its therapeutic properties in the manufacturing of a drug. Who did it belong to – the man, the hospital, or the pharmaceutical company? In a case such as this, the lack of designation as thing ends up preventing the body part from obtaining a stable legal definition. On the other hand, the argument that the nature of a bodily organ changes after it has been separated from the body (or even the entire body after death), making it pass from the regime of person to that of thing, remains unconvincing. If a body or a part of it has ever been a person, it will continue to be so under any condition; and if, instead, at a certain time it has become a thing, then it was so from the beginning.[5]

No matter what angle we consider the question from, we remain embroiled in a series of paradoxes that seem to hinder us from arriving at a resolution. The notion that the body can be reduced to a thing is contrary to our sensibility, but the idea that the body is always equivalent to the person goes against logic. The impossibility of solving the problem evidently arises from a legal terminology that is still based on the old division between persons and things – one that no longer stands in the face of the extraordinary transformations that we are currently undergoing. The way the human body protrudes into both categories testifies to their conceptual inadequacy. Not only is it impossible to classify the body as a person or a thing, the perpetually new challenges that the human body poses to the law show that it is in urgent need of a new formulation. In reality, in the course of the last few decades, jurisprudence has been gradually opening its doors to the life that it shut out of its borders for so long. Starting in the mid-1900s, for example, the laws regulating the transfusion of blood – something, it turned out, that could not be classified as a person or a thing – introduced the *bios* into the formalized space of the law. Subsequent legislation on the surgical removal of organs for transplant from the corpses of people who did not declare their contrary wishes when they were alive broke the exclusive relationship between body and individual, making the body a sort of collective good. The proposal adopted in 1998 by the United Nations General Assembly to qualify the human genome as a "common heritage of mankind" advanced this process even further. But the crucial development came with the rapid growth of biotechnologies. The increasingly widespread practice of transplantation has made even the identification between body and person unfeasible. Without overlooking the commercial currents in the exchange of human organs, the general line of reasoning that has taken hold goes in the direction of a social circulation of the body outside the market of things, but also beyond the boundaries of the person.[6]

This change should not be interpreted as a revocation of what has been proclaimed by various factions as "the sanctity of life." Rather, it can be seen as a transfer of the body from the sphere of the proper to that of the common, due to the transformation of both these terms. The fact that the concept of life has been radically redefined after the discovery of the genome is all too obvious. But a similar change has also affected the notion of sanctity. In point of fact, in ancient Roman law sacred things (*res sacrae*) were linked with things that were common to all (*res communes*). Although they enjoyed a different status, they shared the condition of things that were not part of one's property (*extra patrimonium*) and that were outside commerce (*extra commercium*). In Gaius' *Institutions*, the first distinction between things that "either form part of our property or do not form part of it" is followed by that between things subject to divine right (*res divini juris*) and things subject to human right (*res humani iuris*). The latter are subdivided in their turn into public (*publicae*) and private (*privatae*). Following a procedure typical of Roman law, each category then splits into further ramifications. Thus, the *res publicae* do not coincide with the *res communes*. While common things, such as air or water, do not belong to anyone, public things, such as theaters or markets, are under the co-ownership of the citizens. In turn, the *res divini juris* are divided into *sacrae*, consecrated to worship; *religiosae*, including tombs, corpses, and ashes; and *sanctae*, such as the walls and the gates of the city. However, despite their differences, all divine things share the characteristic with public things of not being appropriable by individuals. This is so much the case that in both the Republican and Imperial ages, sacred things and public things occupied a legally homogeneous sphere: they were subject to the same administrative, fiscal, and criminal regimes, in the sense that they were protected by the same prohibitions. This is not because what was once public was now considered sacred; rather, since the sacred could not be considered private, it was perceived as public.

Something of the sort can be said for the human body, in a way that is comparable to the dimension of the *res sacrae*.[7] Because the body does not coincide with the mask of the person, and yet cannot be reduced to the appropriability of the thing, it falls under the third genus consisting of the *res sacra*. Belonging neither to the state nor to the Church, nor exclusively to the person that dwells inside it, the body owes its inviolability to the fact that it is eminently common. This is not only in the obvious sense that everyone has a body, but also in the more powerful sense that each human body is the patrimony of humanity as a whole. The body is not a thing to be exploited or consumed, of course, but neither is it, strictly speaking, a legal person. As Simone Weil pointed out in the essay we mentioned previously, what is sacred in the human body is not its personal core, but, on the contrary, its impersonal nucleus: "What is sacred, far from being the person, is what, in a human being, is impersonal in him."[8] In opposition to all defenses of personhood, which at the time were reaching their apogee, Weil revindicated what lies beyond, but also before personhood. The fact that she was referring specifically to the body, taken in its

107

absolute inviolability, is made explicit by a glaring example that she offers slightly earlier:

> I see a passer-by in the street. He has long arms, blue eyes, and a mind whose thoughts I do not know, but perhaps they are commonplace. [. . .] If it were the human personality in him that was sacred to me, I could easily put out his eyes. As a blind man he would be exactly as much a human personality as before. I should not have touched the person in him at all. I should have destroyed nothing but his eyes.[9]

The Power of the Body

While the law tends to omit the body, philosophy includes it in its framework, but in the form of the body's subordination. Without repeating the exclusionary gesture of Platonic metaphysics, and yet not entirely foregoing it, modern thought places the body under the rubric of *object*. The body is what the subject recognizes inside itself, as different from itself. To be able to deal with the body, the subject must separate itself from the body and keep it at a distance. Descartes' position on this is exemplary. Indeed, his entire philosophy can be regarded as a series of reflections on the body, but always from a point of view lying outside it, and defined precisely by this exteriority. To talk about 'dualism' in Descartes' thought risks perpetuating an interpretative stereotype. Yet, even if we keep the relationship between mind and body continually in sight, the predominance of separation over unity remains irrefutable. As he explains in one of the most famous passages in his *Discourse on the Method*, "Accordingly this 'I' – that is, the soul by which I am what I am – is entirely distinct from the body, and indeed is easier to know than the body, and would not fail to be whatever it is, even if the body did not exist."[10] Positing the nonexistence of the body as an *argumentum ad absurdum* does not attenuate the negative relation that it establishes between the two substances. The relation between the *res cogitans* and the *res extensa* is an insurmountable division. Not only is the mind not coextensive with the body, in order to recognize itself in its own essential principle, the mind must make itself autonomous from the body. The moment knowledge questions its own legitimacy, its entire existence seems to contract into the point of an incorporeal consciousness. Its privileged expression – because there is nothing better to strip things down into an ideal set of characteristics that thwarts their reality – is mathematics. Mathematical knowledge, the true science of the soul, testifies to the absolute primacy of reason over body: while the latter is always divisible and particular, the former is indivisible and universal. If the body is a machine, reason is the command point that controls its functioning from the outside. There is an infinite hierarchical difference between the two substances out of which human beings are composed.

But this paradigm, widely prevalent in modern thought, is not the only one to characterize it. Another paradigm accompanies the first, juxtaposed to it, that is less continuous and consistent, recognizable specifically by the inverted power relations between mind and body.[11] It originates from the thought of Spinoza. The passage that he completed from Descartes' dual substance to the two modes (thinking and extended) of a single substance opened up an untraveled path. For Spinoza, a mind deprived of a body is inconceivable; indeed, the body is the sole object of the mind: "the object of the idea constituting the human mind is the body – i.e., a definite mode of extension actually existing, and nothing else."[12] The knowledge that for Descartes was made possible by the separation of mind from body now depends on their unassailable unity. One causes the expansion or contraction of the other. Between the two, it is precisely the outlook of the body, one might say, that is refracted productively through the functioning of the mind: "For as the body is more capable of being affected in many ways and of affecting external bodies in many ways, so the mind is more capable of thinking."[13] The Cartesian perspective of a body closed to the intelligence of the world is replaced by the conviction that only through the body can the mind adequately know things. Corporeality, for Spinoza, is the origin of knowledge, the vehicle of experience, the fount of wonder. He continues:

> However, nobody as yet has determined the limits of the body's capabilities [. . .]. [C]lear evidence that the body, solely from the laws of its own nature, can do many things at which its mind is amazed.[14]

Rather than being a simple machine, as Descartes and Hobbes maintained, the body is a weave of symbolic nexuses; only through these can reality take on consistency. The body makes it possible for us to grasp things not in isolation, but as part of the whole complex from which they gain meaning. Subject and object of thought, rigidly separated by Descartes, fit together into the same block of meaning, which arises specifically from their connection. Just as no things exist outside the consciousness that comprehends them, similarly, no consciousnesses exist prior to the constitutive relationship with the world. What lies at the beginning and end of the process is not the illumination of a knowing subject, but the infinite power of life.

Not unsurprisingly, Spinoza deconstructs the exclusionary dispositif of the person right down to its roots. This applies to the divine substance – identical to the impersonal order of the real – as much as it does to the human substance, rescued from the splitting of the Cartesian subject and reconstituted in its ontological fullness. In contrast to the solitude of a *cogito* that is concentrated around its own inner principle, the body's knowledge is revealed as an instrument of connection, a means of sociability, and an aggregating power: "The human body needs for its preservation a great many other bodies."[15] This ontological statement clearly resonates politically. Human beings will flourish only if they combine their bodies into a collective entity that can be called by the name of the "multitude." This is the point where modern thought truly does appear to split off into diverging directions. For Hobbes, the preservation of human beings against the risk of violent death that besets them is ensured by their separation; for Spinoza, on the contrary, it depends on the ability to interweave relationships:

> Men, I repeat, can wish for nothing more excellent for preserving their own being than that they should all be in such harmony in all respects that their minds and bodies should compose, as it were, one mind and one body.[16]

We could be listening to the words of Giambattista Vico, situated at the other pole of modernity's philosophical quadrant, which also address the profound connection between reason and body.[17] In his *New Science*, more than in any other text, what lies at the origin of the world is not the absoluteness of the subject, but the mingling of bodies. It is from their pressure that history originates, with all that this implies in terms of knowledge and power. Nothing is definitively lost regarding that beginning, when the minds of men "were entirely immersed in the senses, buffeted by the passions, buried in the body"[18] – as is demonstrated by the fact that many names of inanimate objects derive from the organs of the body. Even from a linguistic point of view things arise from bodies.

The break with modern thought resulting from these pages cannot be overestimated. Central to them is the changing role of the body. The relative importance of the body with respect to consciousness was altered, but so was the perspective from which this relationship was viewed. The eye of the mind was replaced, or flanked, by that of the body. Ever since "contemplation of the heavens with the bodily eyes" began, narrates Vico, it remained central to human history.[19] Even when contemplation seemed to take the opposite direction, toward increasing abstraction, this remained true. Certainly, humans owe the development of abstraction to the transition from the primitive stage to the rise of civilization. But to this they also owe the crises that periodically embroil them, threatening to take away everything achieved until that point. The cause for this periodic reversion lies in a change in the balance between the "common" and the "proper," tipping the scale toward the latter. But it also points to the breakdown of the connection between reason and body that was established at the dawn of history. The prevailing of reason over body runs parallel to that of the proper over the common, the private over the public, and individual profit over collective interest. This happens when the push for immunity prevails over the passion for community. To protect themselves, human beings compress the power of the body into control apparatuses that bind them to the established orders instituted at various times in history. But, in so doing, they end up losing contact with the sources of life. The only way to rediscover these is to reopen the horizons of the mind to the vitality of the body.

This line of reasoning was brought to fruition by the work of Nietzsche. His radical deconstruction of the categories of modern thought coincided with a thought on and of the body (in the sense that the body thinks because it, too, is animate) that was destined to inaugurate a new language. To the question of whether philosophy has not been more than an incessant *"misunderstanding of the body*,"[20] Zarathustra responds that "there is more reason in your body than in your best wisdom."[21] Contrary to thinkers that Nietzsche defines as disparagers of the body, he rereads the whole history of Europe along "the guiding thread of the body."[22] This primarily concerns the domain of knowledge, whose aim is to control the bodily instincts by disciplining them, but it also concerns the domain of power, increasingly described in terms of biopolitical dynamics. When he observes that "great politics affirm physiology over all other problems,"[23] Nietzsche is referring to the crucial importance assumed by the bodies of individuals and populations in a world that can no longer be interpreted through the modern notions of the sovereign state and individual rights. The politics of bodies, on bodies, in bodies is the only kind that exists – not in opposition to the "spirit," but in a weave that integrates the body into the *bios* as an integral form of life.

The "will to power," an expression that is only too well known, does not refer exclusively to the vital nature of politics – it also points to the political nature of life. The body is the battlefield on which the forces of human beings clash against each other in a relentless struggle: at stake is the very definition of what we are, but also of what we can become. The whole set of protocols that later acquired the name of anthropogenetics – as delicate as they are decisive – are explicitly rooted in Nietzsche's thought. When he wonders why we don't create men the way the Chinese create trees that have pears on one side and roses on the other,[24] the potential dangers contained in these expressions must not be underestimated. But the novelty that they offer compared to a humanistic tradition that had by then been exhausted must also not be overlooked. Although Heidegger would argue in the mid-twentieth century that man is closer to a God than to an animal, since only he is "world-forming," in contrast to the animal, which is "poor in world" and the stone, which is "worldless,"[25] Nietzsche, anticipated by Darwin, reconnected human history to the sphere of nature. Human beings are innately endowed with the capacity to open up a range of possible variations, destined in their turn to retroactively impinge on our genetic makeup: the animal that is human is programmed to continuously change its own programming. From this point of view, technology is not necessarily opposed to nature; in fact, as far as our species is concerned, technology is the fruit of our nature. Every movement of our body and every sound of our voice is technological. Human nature, it has been said,[26] has displayed an originary technicity that we are free to adopt and even called on to develop.

To Exist the Body

The reason the body falls outside the great division between things and persons lies in the fact that it cannot be ascribed to one or the other. As Merleau-Ponty writes, "There are two senses, and two only, of the word 'exist': one exists as a thing or else one exists as a consciousness. The experience of our own body, on the other hand, reveals to us an ambiguous mode of existing."[27] The philosophical importance of the body resides precisely in its ability to stretch the binary order of the Cartesian tradition by directing attention to an entity that cannot be reduced to the categories of subject and object. Although the body is regularly objectified by scientistic attitudes, it protrudes outside the dimension of the object

– an observation affirmed by the entire phenomenological tradition. For Husserl, for example,
'my body' is "the only one of them that is not just
a body but precisely an animate organism";[28] for
Sartre its meaning "is often obscured by the fact
that [. . .] the body is from the start posited as a
certain *thing*";[29] while for Gabriel Marcel "it is
obvious that my body, in that sense, is myself; for
I cannot distinguish myself from it unless I am
willing to reduce it to an object."[30]

Certainly, I can consider my eyes or my hands
a fragment of matter, thereby including them
in the space of external objects, but something
escapes and rebels against this attempt. Between
the two planes there exists an ineffaceable difference: although the object disappears from my
field of vision as soon as I turn my gaze elsewhere,
I cannot stop perceiving my body. It is there, not
in front of me, but with me, bound tightly to
my consciousness in an unbreakable bond. My
body is not what I have, but what I *am*. We
should turn 'to exist' into a transitive verb, sug-
gests Sartre, so that we can say "I exist my body:
this is its first dimension of being."[31] At stake
is a different position in space: instead of being
placed in space like other objects, the body is

the perceptual horizon inside of which these are located. While I may be able to change the angle of view from which I observe an external object from one time to the next, the same does not hold true for my body. I cannot see all of its parts, except in a mirror; nor can I walk all around it. In order to do this, I would have to go outside myself through a second body, one that is independent of the first and that confronts it from outside. But this would make me other than what I am. No matter how hard I attempt to grasp it from the outside, before I do so my body takes hold of me again, because its existence is the precondition of every action I perform. No matter how hard I try to forget it, my body remains there, where it was. And indeed, its "permanence is absolute and is the ground for the relative permanence of disappearing objects, real objects."[32]

This means that the living body does not belong in the material realm of objects, but also that it is the transcendental condition of their existence. If I made my point of view one perspective among others, the entire world that surrounds me would be suddenly blotted out. We perceive the object only because it is "situated [. . .] directly under our hand or gaze," touched,[33] felt, stimulated by the extremities of our bodies: "The look, we said, envelops, palpates, espouses the visible things [. . .] so that finally one cannot say if it is the look or if it is the things that command."[34] The body is what makes the object a thing. In order to be such, a thing among things, the object must be manifest to the sensory organs as something present. But it must also disappear when I detach myself from it, excluding it from my field of vision. What makes it a real thing, and not an imagined object, is the fact that it can also *not* be there. This is how we must interpret Merleau-Ponty's assertion that the body is never an object, because it is precisely that which makes objects possible. The existence of objects is guaranteed by the resistance of my body toward them and vice versa. Consciousness, from this point of view, is tension toward things by means of the body, just as the body is what connects things to consciousness. The two perspectives must be superimposed on each other in a single meaningful block. To move our bodies means to extend toward things, but this is only possible if the body is not one of them. The assertion that the human being is a thing is only acceptable if it refers to something that is the precondition to the existence of any other. As Helmuth Plessner puts it, man experiences himself as a thing and from within a thing that is nevertheless entirely distinct from all other things because he is that particular thing.[35]

Thus, what connects human beings and things is the body. Outside the connection that the body ensures, the two elements are destined to detach from each other in a way that necessarily makes one subordinate to the other. Only from the point of view of the body do they rediscover the original link that was severed by the great division: "the body unites us directly with the things through its own ontogenesis," since things are nothing but "the prolongation of my body and my body is the prolongation of the world."[36] This is not a simple juxtaposition, but a true interpenetration. Only the body is able to fill in the gap that two thousand years of law, theology, and philosophy carved out between things and persons, placing one at the disposition of the other.

In reality we cannot say that phenomenology fully grasps the significance of this contamination between body and thing. This is because the language of Husserl remains in the semantic horizon of the person, despite its projections toward otherness. What he refers to ultimately remains "one's own body," with a predominately spiritual sense. This is what the experience of perception always refers to, in a form that Merleau-Ponty develops and refines but never completely surpasses. The hands that touch each other, or skim things, remain those of a subject that can perceive the other being only thanks to its own inner experience. As much as it is understood and assimilated, the thing remains the object of someone who always relates to it starting from his or her own self. Only when the phenomenological tradition is deconstructed and turned inside-out into its most radical exteriority do body and thing once again intersect and penetrate each other, from a different approach. This happens when the body loses absolute ownership of itself through the mode of the technological prosthesis. Only then does a fragment of the body of others, or a non-bodily thing, turn the human body into a space that cannot be fully appropriated, because it is beyond, or before, the dichotomies between subject and object, internal and external, thought and living body. In the philosophical story of his own heart transplant, Jean-Luc Nancy expresses himself thus:

My heart became my stranger: strange precisely because it was inside. The strangeness could only come from outside because it surged up first on the inside. [. . .] The intrusion of a body foreign to thought. This blank will stay with me like thought itself and its contrary, at one and the same time.[37]

This is the same author who, through the vicissitudes of the body, aimed at the "heart of things."[38] This is an expression that we all use regularly, in the sense of directly confronting the reality of a situation without any filters, but we should try to express it in its most literal sense as well. Just like living beings, things also have a heart, buried in their stillness or in their silent movement: a heart of stone, as they say, but a stone that has no recall of the chill of death. It is a living, pulsing stone, in which ancient or even contemporary experience is concentrated, still palpable, visible, and recognizable – for as long, at least, as *that* thing remains precisely that and nothing else. Whatever else one might say about it, this is no longer possible when things enter into the circuit of serial production, in which, in contrast to the symbolic power that becomes solidified in hand-crafted products, they lose their soul.

But this is only the case as long as they remain items in an inventory, lined up facelessly in a warehouse. As soon as they enter into our homes, discovering a relationship with our bodies, things become special once again, as if each received its own name. This is the paradoxical idea put forward by John Locke and later picked up on by Jorge Luis Borges.[39] From that moment on we begin to feel tied to them by a bond that goes far beyond their market price. These things bear imprinted on them the touch of our hands, the marks of our gaze, the traces of our experience.[40] If it is "things that make us smart,"[41] then layered in them are meanings that cannot be reduced to cognitive terms. These meanings constitute the symbolic node in which their life is intertwined with ours. Just as bodies give life to things, similarly things mold bodies. Pier Paolo Pasolini once wrote that "The education given to a boy by things, by objects, by physical reality [. . .] make that boy corporeally what he is and what he will be all his life. What has to be educated is his flesh as the mould of his spirit."[42]

This secret dialog between us and things, the way they enter deeply into our lives, often transforming them, is also what Ludwig Wittgenstein alluded to in his *Philosophical Investigations* when he stated that "The chair is thinking to itself."[43] To say that a thing thinks, following the assonance between *Ding* and *Denken* that Hegel once noted, does not mean to make an idol of it, an object of fetishism. What is intended, rather, is that we also think by means of the thing; as Henri Bergson argued, they are the place out of which our perceptions arise.[44] Things affect us, at least as much as we affect them. Just as things cannot live without us, we cannot live without them. Certainly, it can be argued that no civilization destroys things as easily as ours does. They often strike us as superseded or depreciated even before they are used. Not surprisingly, after long trying to build things that are indestructible, today we seek to create ones that are naturally perishable, like plastic, for example, which we now prefer to be biodegradable.

But there are things that resist this force of disintegration. There are things that remain valuable – for some, it is a jewel, for others, a piece of clothing, for others still, a book. Or there is something even tinier and apparently more insignificant, like a piece of string, a bit of fabric or a newspaper cutting that comes to the forefront of our oneiric and real existence, from

Ranier Maria Rilke to Walter Benjamin. In *The Book of Disquiet*, the Portuguese poet Fernando Pessoa confesses his love for the slightest, most unimportant of things that smack of unreality,[45] but which allow us to brush up against the mystery of existence. No one grasped this connection between the life of humans and the life of things better than Eugenio Montale when in his poem on "Dora Markus" he wrote:

> I don't know how you endure exhausted
> in this pool
> of indifference that is your heart; perhaps
> you're saved by an amulet that you keep
> near your lipstick,
> your powder puff, your nail file: a white ivory
> mouse; and so you exist![46]

The Soul of Things

According to a popular theory, communities characterized mainly by the relationship between people have been replaced by individualistic social systems oriented instead toward the relationship between people and things. This is true only if you reduce the role of things to the commercial one of objects of exchange that are opposed to the people who make use of them. This is exactly what Marcel Mauss remarks on:

> We live in societies that draw a strict distinction [. . .] between real rights and personal rights, things and persons. Such a separation is basic: it constitutes the essential condition for a part of our system of property, transfer, and exchange.[47]

This binary dispositif, which is anything but originary, overlays other forms of relationship – such as those of the gift or potlatch "in which persons and things merge" –[48] and stamps them out. Persisting for a long time in Indian and Germanic areas, traces of these other forms are also to be found in ancient Roman law, specifically in the practice of the *nexum* – the institution we mentioned earlier that places the body of insolvent debtors at the full disposition of their creditors. Rather than a passive object of transaction, even after being passed into other hands, the *res* remains linked to the first owner by a bond that obligates the new owner until he is released by fulfilling the terms of the contract. Until then, the contracting party remains *reus* (*res*

+ *os*, the ancient genitive suffix), in other words, literally "possessed by the thing."[49] As soon as the *res* is acquired, the recipient acknowledges that he is at the disposition of the donor until payment, committing his own body as guarantee. In short, contravening the logic of the great division, the dynamic of gift exchange revolves around the principle of the personality of the thing.

When the Romans began to distinguish between real rights and personal rights, separating persons and things, the economy of the gift continued to be practiced in cultural spheres that remained outside commercial practices. What they all share is a conception that attributes a soul to things given, received, and returned. Far from being separate from the sphere of persons, things appear to be an integral part, to the point of exerting a powerful action on them: "things have special powers and form part of human persons."[50] They enter into what is at the same time both a protective and a risky relationship with the people who exchange them, ultimately leaving a mark on their fortunes. In Brahman cultures, the thing even speaks in first person – give me, it asks the donor, receive me, it enjoins the recipient, and then give me back, if you want to live again. The locus where the power of the thing exerts itself, even before its metamorphosis into personhood, is the body of the individuals and communities in which it takes up membership.

In this regard, Mauss recalls the *hau*, the spirit of things (*taonga*) given in Maori society, a ritual that has aroused the curiosity of critics:

> Let us suppose that you possess a certain article (*taonga*) and that you give me this article. [. . .] Now, I give this article to a third person who after a certain lapse of time, decides to give me something as payment in return (*utu*). He makes a present to me of something (*taonga*). Now, this *taonga* that he gives me is the spirit (*hau*) of the *taonga* I had received from you and that I had given to *him*. The *taonga* that I received for these *taonga* (which came from you) must be returned to you."[51]

The most striking aspect of this ritual practice is its triadic structure.[52] Rather than simply returning the thing received, the recipient passes it on to a third person, who gives him back another thing in exchange, intended in its turn for the first donor. Why is there this extra step, which complicates the direct relationship between giving and receiving? There has to be a slight differential gap created between what is given and what is received in order to avoid the absolute equivalence of the market economy. This is the only way to respect the singularity of the thing, its specific symbolic charge, and to avoid generalizing it in the logic of commerce. Not only that, but it creates a social relationship that goes beyond the dyadic one to espouse a larger circle involving the entire community. This is the principle that presided for an incredibly long time over both the voluntary and mandatory circulation of wealth, tributes, and gifts in a large part of the world. Central to it is the rejection of the binary dichotomy between people and things:

> In short, this represents an intermingling. Souls are mixed with things; things with souls. Lives are mingled together, and this is how, among persons and things so intermingled, each emerges from their own sphere and mixes together.[53]

What allows and causes this intermixture is the ambiguousness of the body. It is the silent mechanism that facilitates the passage from one code to the other through the chain of symbols engendered by its very presence.[54] The body stops the symbols from being separated from things and from blocking the social circulation into a transcendental type of hierarchical order in which the absolute domination of people over things is reflected in the domination of some people over others, who are also reduced to things. It is remarkable that this perspective – found in ancient societies without being reflected on – has come back into contemporary discussion at a time when the bivalent logic of modernity is opening up to other paradigms, ones that previously nurtured it from within but are now freed to surface on its outer edges. I am referring to the oblique relation between origins and fulfillment, or between the ancient and the present, so familiar to Nietzsche and Benjamin, which leads the gaze of the historian beyond the most obvious thresholds of discontinuity, and that of the philosopher even more.

At its heart there stands the current impact of technology on things that are no longer only objects, and of subjects who are increasingly difficult to confine inside the dispositif of the person. In the early 1950s, Gilbert Simondon had already begun talking about "technical objects" as the mediating ground between human beings and nature.[55] They bear imprinted within them the signs of intelligence needed to solve the problems that have periodically loomed on the human horizon. Far from being simple tools limited to accomplishing the immediate tasks of manual labor, they hold a quantity of information that makes them charged with social effectiveness. Not unlike Mauss' *hau*, Simondon's *objet technique* has a subjective component that, rather than submitting us to its magic power, enhances our creative capacity. Only a misunderstood anthropocentrism prevents us from seizing on and using what we ourselves have developed and mobilized in a form – both objective and subjective – that continues to live inside the thing as much as it does inside us. This awareness has nothing to do with a sort of facile antihumanism, generally based on an ignorance of the consequential relevance of the great humanistic tradition that arose out of the Italian Renaissance. The idea that man has no pre-established essence, apart from that of being "self-fashioning" and continually changing his nature, is the kernel of Pico della Mirandola's celebrated "Oration on the Dignity of Man."

Of course, our own bodies constitute the

floating bridge that connects us to technical objects. This means not only the mind, from which they derive their functional and symbolic characteristics, but also the bodily signs that are deposited in them in the act of their invention. The passage from one set of hands to the next by those who have used them creates a continuous flow that goes beyond the individual to involve the "transindividual" dimension to which Simondon dedicated his greatest work.[56] To receive a technical object from those who invented and used it means to reconstruct a social chain not that dissimilar to what anthropologists believe they have discovered in the gifting rituals of "peoples without history." The metapolitical implication that Simondon derives from this characterization of the technical object is hardly overlooked. Only when the technical object is emancipated from its servile reduction to a mere tool in the hands of humans will the domination also come to an end of those who control technology over those who are limited to enduring it.

It is not against the machine that humankind must turn in order to shore up its humanistic reserve. We are enslaved by the machine only when machines are enslaved by the community [. . .]. Traditional humanism remained abstract when it defined the power of self-determination as only belonging to the citizens instead of to the slaves.[57]

Bruno Latour comes to a similar conclusion a few decades later when he proposes the notion of "a parliament of things" to overcome the great modern division between nature and society.[58] In his view, although modernity theoretically negated hybrids, located at the point of intersection between "quasi-subjects" and "quasi-objects," it actually made ample use of them. But this distinction running along the thread of the body, which remained a fault line in the modern era, yawned open into a full-fledged crevasse as the period drew to a close. A sort of beneficial counter effect has taken place, arising in contrast to the bipolar obsession: the more persons are separated from things, the more things take on human characteristics over time. The dividing line that long opposed scientific objects to political subjects has now been broken down by phenomena constituted mid-way between nature and history, science and politics, persons and things: "Yet the human, as we now understand, cannot be grasped and saved unless that other part of itself, the share of things, is restored to it."[59] Not only are objects intermingled with human elements, solidified and made interchangeable for others, people are in their turn traversed by information, codes, and flows arising from the continuous use of technical objects. In perceptual and cognitive terms, neither the psychological nor the physiological features of humans are independent of their manipulation of things, to the point that humans have been defined "artifacts of their artifacts."[60]

The thinker who has spoken the most about this ancient and postmodern encounter between persons who are no longer persons with things that are no longer things is Peter Sloterdjik. Starting from the work of Gottard Günther on a new social ontology,[61] Sloterdjik has developed a sort of anthropotechnics on the confine of mutual connivance between humans and things. Without breaking with the Heideggerian paradigm, but realigning it, so to speak, from Being to beings, he contrasts the dangers of "allotechnics" to the unprecedented resources offered by a "homeotechnics." The difference between the two lies in the fact that while the first is aimed at the absolute domination of nature, the second mimics its creative processes. The crux of his vision lies, once again, in the logic of a new alliance that goes beyond the great division between persons and things. Intelligent machines, works of art, computers, and all other types of artifacts usher us into a dimension that cuts across their supposed division:

> Compared to devices of this type, the fundamental conceptual division (used in the most developed cultures) between soul and thing, spirit and matter, subject and object, freedom and mechanicism, will no longer gain any traction.[62]

For an untold time that has yet to end, we have attributed the same superabundant quality to persons that we have taken away from things. The time has come to rebalance relations. But even before doing that, we need to break through the barrier that has divided the world between opposing species. Without denying the disquieting nature of the revolution we are currently undergoing – especially when technology penetrates our bodies, upsetting orders that have existed for thousands of years – the importance of the shift remains.

Perhaps for the first time since the disappearance of ancient societies, things have come back to interpellate us directly. A whole system of meaning is being rocked, rotating around its own axis, and landing in a different position: "After the abolition of slavery in the nineteenth century," concludes Sloterdijlk, "a widespread disintegration of the ancient domination is looming for the twenty-first or twenty-second century."[63] Through what conflicts will this take place, and with what consequences? "In questions like these the conviction being voiced is that modern thought will be incapable of an ethics until it clarifies its logic and its ontology."[64]

Political Bodies

Unlike law and philosophy, politics has always maintained an intrinsic relationship with the body. The "body politic," moreover, is one of the oldest figures in the Western tradition. Its first occurrences date back as early as ancient Greek thought, however, it was in the Early Middle Ages that it took on special importance. The state order was compared to a living body that is organic and differentiated into mutually coordinated functions. Of course, the relationship between the various members of the body, representing the various social strata, changed according to the intentions of whoever employed the metaphor. Whether the main organ on which the functioning of all of the other organs depended was the head, the soul, or the heart was not irrelevant to its overall significance. For example, in John of Salisbury's *Policraticus*, the hegemony of the head was somehow balanced by the interrelation of the other parts; in Hobbes' *Leviathan*, however, the unyielding command of the soul over the rest of the body expressed the transition to an absolutist conception centered on the sovereign's dominion. Rousseau, instead, arguing that "we receive each member as an indivisible part of the whole,"[65] gave the metaphor an egalitarian outcome, brought to completion by Joseph Sieyès through the identification of the body of the French nation with the Third Estate.

The most striking feature about this variety of versions is the binary division that gets established in each of them between the personal element of sovereign control and the impersonal structure of the bodily physiology. This explains why at a certain moment, starting with Hobbes, the semantics of the machine were able to over-lap with that of the body without distorting the meaning of the metaphor. However, this did not cancel out a residual gap between the two polari-ties. This is demonstrated by the fact that the term "body" could refer to the whole of the organism as well as to the part lying below the head. We know that this duality arose out of the dogma of Christ's dual nature. Just as the entire body of Christianity did not fully correspond to the body of Christ, also divided in its turn into two parts, similarly the body politic never corresponded entirely to that of the sovereign. Even where full integration between the two was assumed, the lack of correspondence never disappeared completely. This binarism is recognizable in rep-resentative democracies, in the never completely bridged dissymmetry between sovereignty and representation. The very notion of the "people" bears within it two different and potentially con-flicting meanings. It indicates at the same time the totality of the citizenry and its less wealthy part: the nation-people and the plebeian-people. As often happens in the political-theological idiom that we still use, the same concept includes the part that in other respects it excludes. The

entire Western political dynamic can be interpreted as the unrelenting tension between these
two polarities – as an attempt to unify the body
politic or the people, on the one hand, by excluding its low part and, on the other, by eliminating
the differential threshold that divides the low part
from the high part.

In the transition that took place at a certain
point from the sovereign regime to the biopolitical regime, this contradiction began to be even
more marked. It is as if what had been a metaphor
– that of the body politic – materialized, taking
on a body itself. These are exactly the terms used
by the first thinker who analyzed this turn of
events: "The social 'body' ceased to be a simple
juridico-political metaphor (like the one in the
Leviathan) and became a biological reality and
a field for medical intervention."[66] Certainly,
the *bios* has always been an object of political
interest and intervention. But what up to a certain point was filtered by a series of mediations
started to become a direct relationship. From
then on, human life as a framework of political
action became the central focus – it became the
business of government, just as politics became
the government of life. The growing role of

social medicine, directly aimed at the body of the population, reflected the significance of this transition. Thus, commenting on the Prussian health system, Michel Foucault could assert that "it was not the workers' bodies that interested this public health administration, but the bodies of individuals insofar as they combined to constitute the state."[67] This led to a dual, interlinking process on the basis of which medicine became more politicized while politics became increasingly modeled on medical knowledge. This was a decisive turning point in the domain of power, but one that had significant effects in that of knowledge as well. When the living body of individuals and populations became the privileged object, political practice began to evade ancient and modern legal categories of thought. The mechanisms of power took charge of "men's existence, men as living bodies," however, "it was life more than the law that became the issue of political struggles."[68]

This does not mean, however, that the chasm that cut through the political concepts of modernity narrowed. On the contrary, it gaped even wider. When the body became the content rather than the metaphorical signifier of the political order, the fracture that separated the body from the head in the sovereign regime extended even deeper inside it. The exclusion (in addition to the rights) that was created as a consequence had the potential to affect its very biological survival, as happened repeatedly over the course of the twentieth century. This was especially the case under Nazism, which transformed the medical care of life into a sort of lethal surgery aimed at saving the body politic, by removing the part that it considered to be infected. But although biopolitics is always at risk of reversing itself into a form of thanatopolitics, this does not mean that the two are necessarily identical. A politics *of* life always comes as a reaction to a politics focused *on* life. The human body is central to this conflict. While it is the object of control and exploitation, since all forms of power produce resistance, it is also the subject of revolt. As Foucault points out, "against this power that was still new in the nineteenth century, the forces that resisted relied for support on the very thing that it invested, that is on life and man as a living being"; similarly, "life as a political object was in a sense taken at face value and turned back against the system that was bent on controlling it."[69] While the body has always been the ground where persons pass into things, it is also the point of resistance that opposes this passage – not in the sense of a return from thing to person, but as a rejection of the dichotomous order that has always organized the relationship between the two.

In our contemporary biopolitical regime, the mechanism that unifies life through its internal rupture seems to have been jammed. It is as if the two bodies of the king had diverged into a form that can no longer be reunited, and they lie, unreconciled, face to face, as they did in Shakespeare's *Richard II*. What is crumbling is the integration between personal power and impersonal functioning that for four centuries produced the modern state. In the old model, body and head, sovereign and people, charisma and office had long been fused into an institutional unity. During the last century political parties served as its essential cogs and wheels. Today this great model of discipline has gone literally to pieces. Under the combined pressure of globalization and the technological revolution, the leader's persona is gaining prominence, both in political parties and in the government of our democracies, and becoming increasingly autonomous from the institutional apparatus on which it depends.[70] But this emancipation of the leader or the premier from the body politic is to the benefit of his or her physical body, now at center stage, revealed in its most intimate creases. Power has become recognizable in the leader's body – in his or her face, gestures and words – stripped of any mediation. It is difficult to say what the effects will be of this transition into the biopolitical whose genesis can be seen in the 1930s and whose development characterizes the society of spectacle. It is certainly the cause and effect of a withdrawal of politics from the *res publica* as active participation, and of a populist syndrome that has spared no political force. Moreover, with the relentless sensationalism of politics, the public dimension is becoming increasingly confused with the private, to the point that is difficult to distinguish between them.

What is perhaps of most interest is the dynamic that arises at the other pole of the social quadrant – in the part of the political body lying below the head that is now independent of it. While the body and the person of the leader correspond perfectly in the head, with no gaps or differences, in the lower part, the body has acquired an intensely impersonal value. This part is made up of the living bodies of those who feel they are no longer represented by the institutions, defying all interpretative categories. Whatever form of democracy awaits us, it is highly unlikely that it can be entirely contained within the current channels of representation – something of the body politic remains outside their confines. When masses of people crowd into the public squares across half the world, as is happening today, something is revealed that exists prior even to their demands. Before even being uttered, their words are embodied in bodies that move in unison, with the same rhythm, in a single wave of emotion. As much as the Internet can function as a place for mobilization, without living bodies connected together by the same energy, not even it can be the new political subject of the future. Ever since the statement "we, the people" was first pronounced in the founding event of the first modern democracy, it has had a performative character – it has the effect of creating what it declares. Since then, every linguistic act that seeks to have an impact on the political scene requires a mouth and a throat – the breath of bodies close enough to hear what the other says and to see what everyone can see. Hannah Arendt believed that there must be a public space in order for politics to exist. But she failed to add that this space must be filled by living bodies united by the same protests or by the same demands.[71] Still lacking adequate organizational forms, the bodies of men and women are pressing against the edges of our political systems. They seek to transform the systems into a form that cannot be reduced to the dichotomies that the modern political order has long produced. The outcome of these dynamics remains uncertain, but what is striking about them is the radical novelty that they introduce into our history. Foreign to both the semantics of the person and to those of the thing, the living body of increasingly vast multitudes demands a radical renewal of the vocabularies of politics, law, and philosophy. In the coming years we will see whether these institutions will be able to respond, or whether they will shut themselves up in self-defense before definitively imploding.

Notes

1 Persons

1 *The Institutes of Gaius. Parts One and Two*, ed. Francis de Zulueta, 2 vols. Clarendon Press, Oxford 1946. http://faculty.cua.edu/pennington/law508/roman law/ GaiusInstitutesEnglish.htm. Commentary I, 8: "(8) All the *ius* which we make use of has reference either to persons, to things, or to actions."

2 Jorge Luis Borges, "Things," in *Selected Poems*, ed. Alexander Coleman, Penguin Books, New York/ London 2000, p. 277.

3 Aristotle, *Politics* I, 4, 1253b–1254a. *Aristotle in 23 Volumes*, vol. 21, trans. H. Rackham, Harvard University Press, Cambridge, MA, William Heinemann Ltd., London 1944.

4 For a different treatment of the same question, see Emanuele Coccia's *Il bene nelle cose*, il Mulino, Bologna 2014, as well as Mary Douglas and Baron C.

Isherwood, *The World of Goods*, Routledge, New York 1996.

5 Elias Canetti, *Crowds and Power*, trans. Carol Stewart, Continuum, New York 1978, p. 204.

6 For a general discussion on the *res* in ancient Roman law, see Mario Bretone, *I fondamenti del diritto romano. Le cose e la natura*, Laterza, Rome–Bari 2001, especially pp. 46ff.

7 Gaius, *Institutions*, IV, 16.

8 Canetti, *Crowds and Power*, p. 140.

9 See Yan Thomas, *Les Opérations du droit*, ed. M.-A. Hermitte and P. Napoli, Gallimard, Paris 2011, pp. 27ff.

10 Gaius, *Institutions*, 4.16.

11 See Philippe Simonnot, *Les personnes et les choses*, Les Belles Lettres, Paris 2004, pp. 129ff.

12 See Rudolf von Jhering, *Geist des römischen Rechts auf den verschiedenen Stufen seiner Entwicklung* (1852–65), Scientia Verlag, Aalen 1993.

13 On the notion of 'person' in ancient Rome, see *Homo, caput, persona. La costruzione giuridica dell'identità nell'esperienza giuridica romana*, ed. A. Corbino, M. Humbert, G. Negri, Iuss Press, Pavia 2010; and E. Stolfi, *Il diritto, la genealogia, la storia. Itinerari,* il Mulino, Bologna 2010, pp. 139ff.

14 Nietzsche, "On the Genealogy of Morals," in *Basic Writings*, trans. Walter Kaufmann, Random House, Modern Library edn., New York 2000, p. 506.

15 Simone Weil, "Human Personality," in *Selected Essays 1934–1943*, trans. Richard Rees, Oxford University Press, Oxford 1962, p. 62; *Antologia del pensiero*

impolitico, ed. Roberto Esposito, Bruno Mondadori, Milan 1996, p. 76.

16 See Roberto Esposito, *Third Person. Politics of life and philosophy of the impersonal*, trans. Zakiya Hanafi, Polity Books, Cambridge 2012.

17 Jacques Maritain, *The Rights of Man and Natural Law*, trans. Doris C. Anson, Gordian Press, New York 1971, p. 55 and 65.

18 Robert Joseph Pothier, *Traité des personnes et des choses*, in *Œuvres de Pothier*, vol. 9, ed. M. Bugnet, Paris 1846.

19 See Roberto Esposito, *Due. La macchina della teologia politica e il posto del pensiero*, Einaudi, Turin 2013; English version, forthcoming: *Two. The Machine of Political-Theology and the Place of Thought*, trans. Zakiya Hanafi, Fordham University Press, Bronx, New York.

20 Augustine, *On the Holy Trinity*, XI, 1, 1, from *A Select Library of the Nicene and Post-Nicene Fathers of the Christian Church. Vol. III St. Augustin on the Holy Trinity, Doctrinal Treatises, Moral Treatises*, ed. Philip Schaff, The Christian Literature Co., Buffalo 1887.

21 *The Summa Theologica of St. Thomas Aquinas*, Second and Revised Edition, 1920. Literally trans. Fathers of the English Dominican Province. Online Edition Copyright © 2008 by Kevin Knight, I, Q. 29, Art. 1.

22 Ernst Kantorowicz, *The King's Two Bodies. A Study in Mediaeval Political Theology*, Princeton University Press, Princeton NJ 1997.

23 William Shakespeare, *Richard II*, in *Works of Shakespeare*, Cambridge University Press, Cambridge 1939, III, 2, pp. 155ff.

24 Kantorowicz, *The King's Two Bodies*, p. 27.

25 Ibid., p. 30.

26 Ibid., p. 41.

27 John Locke, *An Essay Concerning Human Understanding*, Prometheus Books, New York 1995, p. 256.

28 Immanuel Kant, "What Real Progress has Metaphysics Made in Germany since the Time of Leibniz and Wolff?" trans. Peter Heath, in Immanuel Kant, *Theoretical Philosophy After 1781*, Cambridge University Press, Cambridge 2002, p. 362.

29 Immanuel Kant, *The Metaphysics of Morals*, trans. Mary Gregor, Cambridge University Press, Cambridge 1996, p. 56.

30 Ibid., p. 61.

31 Ibid., p. 62.

32 G. W. F. Hegel, *Outlines of the Philosophy of Right*, trans. T. M. Knox, Oxford University Press, Oxford 1952, p. 56.

33 G. W. F. Hegel, *Phenomenology of Spirit*, trans. J. B. Baillie, Digireads.com Publishing, 2009, p. 219.

34 René Descartes, *Meditations on First Philosophy*, trans. John Cottingham, Cambridge University Press, Cambridge 1996, p. 52.

35 John Locke, *Two Treatises of Government*, Cambridge University Press, Cambridge 1988, p. 287.

36 John Stuart Mill, *On Liberty*, Batoche Books, Kitchener 2001, p. 13.

37 Bertrand Lemennicier, "Le corps humain: propriété de l'état ou propriété de soi?" *Droits*, 13 (1991), p. 118 [Tr.: quote translated from the Italian].

38 H. Tristram Engelhardt, *The Foundations of Bioethics*, Oxford University Press, Oxford 1996, p. 240.

39 Ibid., p. 239.
40 Peter Singer, *Writings on an Ethical Life*, HarperCollins, New York 2000, p. 88.
41 Engelhardt, *Foundations of Bioethics*, p. 156
42 Singer, *Writings on an Ethical Life*, p. 204.
43 Ibid., p. 150.

2 Things

1 Martin Heidegger, "The Thing," in Bremen and Freiburg Lectures, *Insight Into That Which Is and Basic Principles of Thinking*, trans. Andrew J. Mitchell, Indiana University Press, Bloomington and Indianapolis, Indiana 2012, pp. 5–22. This citation p. 9.
2 Ibid., p. 9.
3 Plato, *The Republic*, 479c. In *Plato in Twelve Volumes*, vols. 5 and 6, trans. Paul Shorey, Harvard University Press, Cambridge, MA; William Heinemann Ltd., London 1969.
4 Plato, *The Sophist*, 260b–d. In *Plato in Twelve Volumes*, vol. 12, trans. Harold N. Fowler, Harvard University Press, Cambridge, MA; William Heinemann Ltd., London 1921.
5 On this, and generally on the relationship between ontology and nihilism, see the insightful book by Nicola Russo, *La cosa e l'ente. Verso l'ipotesi ontologica*, Cronopio, Naples 2012.
6 Aristotle, *Metaphysics*, IV, 3, 1005b. In *Aristotle in 23 Volumes*, vols. 17, 18, trans. Hugh Tredennick, Harvard University Press, Cambridge, MA; William Heinemann Ltd., London 1933.

7 Aristotle, *Physics*, Books I and II, trans. William Charlton, Clarendon Press, Oxford 1992, 190b, p. 17.

8 Thomas Aquinas, *The Disputed Questions on Truth*, vol. 1, trans. Robert William Mulligan, S. J., Henry Regnery Co., Chicago 1952, Question 2, Art. 2.8, p. 50. See Russo, *La cosa e l'ente*, pp. 149ff.

9 Martin Heidegger, "Age of the World Picture," in *The Question Concerning Technology and Other Essays*, trans. William Lovitt, Garland Publishing, New York/London 1977, pp. 129–30.

10 For the relationship between Roman law and Greek metaphysics, and in general for this characterization of Roman law, see the fundamental book by Aldo Schiavone, *Ius. L'invenzione del diritto in Occidente*, Einaudi, Turin 2005; but also, in a different key, Laurent de Sutter, *Deleuze e la pratica del diritto*, Ombre corte, Verona 2011, pp. 88–9.

11 See Yan Thomas, "La valeur des choses. Le droit romain hors de la religion," in *Annales. Histoire. Sciences Sociales*, 57 (2002), no. 6, pp. 143–62.

12 Michel Foucault, *The Order of Things*, Vintage Books, New York 1994, p. 47.

13 Ferdinand de Saussure, *Writings in General Linguistics*, trans. Carol Sanders and Matthew Pires, Oxford University Press, Oxford 2006, p. 47.

14 As Paolo Virno rightly maintains in his *Saggio sulla negazione. Per un'antropologia linguistica*, Bollati Boringhieri, Turin 2013. See also Massimo Donà, *Sulla negazione*, Bompiani, Milan 2004.

15 G. F. W. Hegel, *The Phenomenology of Spirit* (1807),

trans. J. B. Baillie, Digireads.com Publishing, 2009, p. 54.

16 *G. W. F. Hegel and the Human Spirit. A translation of the Jena Lectures on the Philosophy of Spirit (1805–6)*, trans. Leo Rauch, Wayne State University Press, Detroit 1983, p. 89.

17 Maurice Blanchot, "Literature and the Right to Death," trans. Lydia Davis, reprinted in *The Work of Fire*, Stanford University Press, Stanford 1995, pp. 300–44. This quote p. 323.

18 Ibid., p. 323–4.

19 Ibid., p. 324.

20 Ibid., p. 328.

21 Karl Marx, *Capital: A Critique of Political Economy, Volume 1, First English Edition of 1887*, trans. Samuel Moore and Edward Aveling, ed. Frederick Engels, Progress Publishers, Moscow 1965, p. 46.

22 Ibid., p. 48.

23 Ibid., p. 47.

24 Ibid., p. 50.

25 Ibid., p. 165.

26 Ibid., p. 570; and *Capital*, vol. 3, Progress Publishers, Moscow 1966, p. 606.

27 Walter Benjamin, "The Work of Art in the Age of Mechanical Reproduction," in *Illuminations: Essays and Reflections*, ed. Hannah Arendt, Harcourt, Brace and World, New York 1968, pp. 217–52. This quote p. 221.

28 See Alfred Gell, *Art and Agency. An Anthropological Theory*, Clarendon Press, Oxford 1998.

29 See Günther Anders, *Die Antiquiertheit des Menschen*

[The Outdatedness of Human Beings], 2 vols., Beck, Munich 1980, vol. 2. [Tr. note: translated from the Italian. There is no English translation but it has been translated into Italian as *L'uomo è antiquato*, Bollati Boringhieri, Turin 1992, pp. 50 ff.] Note that his father (W. Stern) had written a three-volume work entitled *Person und Sache*, Barth, Leipzig 1906–1924. For more regarding this topic, see ed. Andrea Borsari, *L'esperienza delle cose*, Marietti, Genoa 1992, p. 8.

30 Simone Weil, *Gravity and Grace*, University of Nebraska Press, Lincoln 1997, p. 210.

31 Martin Heidegger, "Positionality," in Bremen and Freiburg Lectures, *Insight Into That Which Is and Basic Principles of Thinking*, trans. Andrew J. Mitchell, Indiana University Press, Bloomington and Indianapolis, Indiana 2012, pp. 23–43. This quote p. 31.

32 Ibid., p. 36.

33 With diverging perspectives, see Maurizio Ferraris, *Manifesto del nuovo realismo*, Laterza, Rome–Bari 2012, and Gianni Vattimo, *Della realtà*, Garzanti, Milan 2012. See also Luca Taddio, *Verso un nuovo realismo*, Jouvence, Milan 2013.

34 Alain Badiou, *The Century*, trans. Alberto Toscano, Polity, Cambridge 2007.

35 See Mario Perniola, *La società dei simulacri*, Cappelli, Bologna 1980.

36 Jean Baudrillard, *The Transparency of Evil. Essays on Extreme Phenomena*, trans. James Benedict, Verso, London 1993, p. 6.

37 Ibid., p. 7.

38 Jean Baudrillard, *The Intelligence of Evil or the Lucidity Pact*, trans. Chris Turner, Berg, Oxford 2005, p. 26.

39 Jacques Lacan, *The Seminar of Jacques Lacan Book VII. The Ethics of Psychoanalysis 1959–1960*, trans. Dennis Porter, W. W. Norton and Company, New York/London 1992, p. 45.

40 Ibid., p. 46.

41 Ibid., p. 46.

42 Jacques Lacan, *Ecrits. The First Complete Edition in English*, trans. Bruce Fink, W. W. Norton and Company, New York/London 2007, p. 724.

43 See Massimo Recalcati, *Sull'odio*, Bruno Mondadori, Milan 2004, p. 351, and more generally, his dense monography on Lacan, *Jacques Lacan. Desiderio, godimento, soggettivazione*, vol. I, R. Cortina, Milan 2012. On the difference between reality and the Real, see also by Recalcati, *Il sonno della realtà e il trauma del reale*, in M. De Caro and M. Ferraris (eds.), *Bentornata realtà*, Einaudi, Turin 2012, pp. 191–206.

44 See Slavoj Žižek, *Welcome to the Desert of the Real*, Verso, London/New York 2012.

3 Bodies

1 Immanuel Kant, *Lectures on Ethics*, trans. Peter Heath, Cambridge University Press, Cambridge 1997, p. 157.

2 See Stefano Rodotà, *La vita e le regole. Tra diritto e non diritto*, Feltrinelli, Milan 2006, pp. 73ff.

3 Pierre Legendre, *L'inestimable objet de la transmission*, Fayard, Paris 1985, p. 28. [Tr. note: translated from the French.]

4 In this regard, see Jean-Pierre Baud, *L'affaire de la main volée. Une histoire juridique du corps*, Éditions du Seuil, Paris 1993.

5 A useful redefinition of the question can be found in G. Cricenti, *I diritti sul corpo,* Jovene, Naples 2008.

6 See C. Crignon-De Oliveira and M. Gaille-Nikodimov, *À qui appartient le corps humain,* Les Belles Lettres, Paris 2008, pp. 99ff.

7 On the topic of the sacred in relation to Roman law, see L. Garofalo, *Biopolitica e diritto romano*, Jovene, Naples 2009; see also ed. Garofalo, *Sacertà e repressione criminale in Roma arcaica,* Jovene, Naples 2013.

8 Simone Weil, "Human Personality" in *Simone Weil: An Anthology*, ed. Sian Miles, Grove Press, New York 1986, p. 54.

9 Ibid., pp. 50–1.

10 René Descartes, *Discourse on the Method*, in *Selected Philosophical Writings*, trans. John Cottingham, Cambridge University Press, Cambridge 1988, pp. 30–57. This quote p. 36.

11 For a philosophical genealogy of the body, see Umberto Galimberti, *Il corpo,* Feltrinelli, Milan 1983; Michela Marzano, *Philosophie du corps,* Presses Universitaires de France, Paris 2007.

12 Benedict de Spinoza, *The Ethics* in *Complete Works*, trans. Samuel Shirley, ed. Michael L. Morgan, Hackett Publishing Company, Indianapolis, IN 2002, p. 251.

13 Ibid., p. 361.

14 Ibid., p. 280.

15 Ibid., p. 255.

16 Ibid., p. 331.

17 On the relationship between Spinoza and Vico as regards the semantics of the body, see B. de Giovanni, "'Corpo' e 'ragione' in Spinoza e Vico," in Biagio de Giovanni, Roberto Esposito, and Giuseppe Zarone, *Divenire della ragione moderna. Cartesio, Spinoza, Vico*, Liguori, Naples 1981, pp. 94–165.

18 Giambattista Vico, *The New Science*, trans. Thomas Goddard Bergin and Max Harold Fisch, Cornell University Press, Ithaca, New York 1948, p. 106.

19 Ibid., p. 110.

20 Friedrich Nietzsche, *Gay Science*, trans. Walter Kaufmann, Vintage Books/Random House, New York 1974, p. 35.

21 Friedrich Niezsche, *Thus Spoke Zarathustra*, trans. Walter Kaufmann, Viking Penguin, New York/London 1966, pp. 34–5.

22 Friedrich Nietzsche, *Writings from the Late Notebooks*, Cambridge University Press, Cambridge 2003, pp. 27, 30, 71.

23 Friedrich Nietzsche, *Frammenti postumi 1888–89*, ed. Sossio Giametta, Adelphi Edizioni, Milan 1986, p. 407. [Tr. note: quote translated from the Italian.]

24 Nietzsche, *Frammenti postumi, 1881–82*, in *Opere*, vol. V, 2, Adelphi, Milan 1965, p. 432. [Tr. note: translated from the Italian.]

25 Martin Heidegger, *The Fundamental Concepts of Metaphysics: world, finitude, solitude*, trans. William McNeill and Nicholas Walker, Indiana University Press, Bloomington and Indianapolis 1995, p. 196.

26 See especially Bernard Stiegler, *Technics and Time*, trans. Richard Beardsworth and George Collins,

Stanford University Press, Stanford, California 2011; see also Roberto Esposito, "Politics and Human Nature," in *Terms of the Political. Community, Immunity, Biopolitics,* trans. Rhiannon Noel Welch, Fordham University Press, Bronx, New York 2013, pp. 88–99.

27 Maurice Merleau-Ponty, *The Phenomenology of Perception,* trans. Colin Smith, Taylor and Francis e-Library, London 2005, p. 178.

28 Edmund Husserl, *Cartesian Meditations,* trans. Dorion Cairns, Martinus Nijhoff Publishers, The Hague/ Boston/London 1982, p. 97.

29 Jean-Paul Sartre, *Being and Nothingness,* trans. Hazel E. Barnes, Washington Square Press, New York 1984, p. 401.

30 Gabriel Marcel, *Being and Having,* trans. Katharine Farrar, Dacre Press, Westminister 1949, p. 14.

31 Jean-Paul Sartre, *Being and Nothingness,* p. 460.

32 Merleau-Ponty, *Phenomenology of Perception,* p. 80.

33 Ibid., p. 78.

34 Maurice Merleau-Ponty, *The Visible and the Invisible,* trans. Alphonso Lingis, Northwestern University Press, Evanston, Illinois 1968, p. 133.

35 See Helmuth Plessner, *Laughing and Crying: A Study of the Limits of Human Behavior,* trans. James Spencer Churchill and Marjorie Grene, Northwestern University Press, Evanston, Illinois 1970.

36 Merleau-Ponty, *The Visible and the Invisible,* pp. 136, 255.

37 Jean-Luc Nancy, "The Intruder," in *Corpus,* trans. Richard A. Rand, Fordham University Press, Bronx, New York 2008, pp. 161–70. This quote p. 163.

38 Jean-Luc Nancy, "The Heart of Things," in *The Birth to Presence*, trans. Brian Holmes and Others, Stanford University Press, Stanford, California 1993, pp. 167–88.

39 Jorge Luis Borges, "The Library of Babel," in *Collected Ficciones*, trans. Andrew Hurley, Allen Lane, The Penguin Press, New York/London 1998, pp. 112–18. For John Lock see *An Essay Concerning Human Understanding*, pp. 409–19.

40 Regarding the "personal" character of things, see especially Remo Bodei, *La vita delle cose*, Laterza, Rome–Bari 2009 (an English edition is forthcoming from Fordham University Press); also by Bodei, *Oggetti e cose*, Consorzio Festival filosofia, Modena 2013. See also, Arjun Appadurai (ed.), *The Social Life of Things*, Cambridge University Press, Cambridge 1986; Bill Brown (ed.), *Things*, University of Chicago Press, Chicago 2004; F. Rigotti, *Il pensiero delle cose*, Apogeo, Milan 2007; D. Miller, *The Comfort of Things*, Polity, Cambridge 2008; Giovanni Starace, *Gli oggetti e la vita*, Donzelli, Rome 2013.

41 Donald A. Norman, *Things That Make Us Smart: Definding Human Attributes in the Age of the Machine*, Perseus Books, New York 1993.

42 Pier Paolo Pasolini, *Lutheran Letters*, trans. Stuart Hood, Carcanet Press, New York 1987, p. 30.

43 Ludwig Wittgenstein, *Philosophical Investigations*, 4th edn., trans. G. E. M. Anscombe, P. M. S. Hacker, and Joachim Shulte, Wiley–Blackwell Publishing, Malden MA-Oxford 2009, p. 121e.

44 For more on the impersonal nature of perception in Bergson, see especially E. Lisciani Petrini, "Fuori della

persona. L''impersonale' in Merleau-Ponty, Bergson e Deleuze," in *Filosofia politica*, 3 (2007), pp. 393–40; more generally, on the role of the body in twentieth-century philosophy, see Lisciani Petrini's *Risonanze. Ascolto, corpo, mondo*, Mimesis, Milan 2007.

45 Fernando Pessoa, *The Book of Disquiet*, trans. Richard Zenith, Penguin Books, London 2001, p. 436.

46 Eugenio Montale, "Dora Markus" in *Le occasioni* (1939), Einaudi, Turin 1996, pp. 58–9. [Tr. note: translated from the Italian.]

47 Marcel Mauss, *The Gift. The Form and Reason for Exchange in Archaic Societies*, trans. W. D. Halls, Routledge Classics, Abingdon 2002, p. 61.

48 Ibid., p. 61.

49 Ibid., p. 67.

50 Ibid., p. 72.

51 Ibid., p. 14.

52 This question is examined critically by Marshall Sahlins in *Stone Age Economics*, Routledge, London 1972.

53 Mauss, *The Gift*, p. 25–6.

54 On this dynamic see J. Gil, "Corpo," in *Enciclopedia*, Einaudi, Turin 1978, vol. III, pp. 1096–161.

55 Gilbert Simondon, *Du mode d'existence des objets techniques* (1958), Aubier, Paris 1989. [Tr. note: an English translation is available of the first part of Simendon's work by Ninian Mellamphy, University of Western Ontario, London 1980.] On this topic, see F. Minazzi, "'Salire sulle proprie spalle?' Simondon e la trasduttività dell'ordine del reale," in *aut aut*, 361 (2014), pp. 110–29.

56 Gilbert Simondon, *L'individuation psychique et*

collective à la lumière des notions de Forme, Potentiel et Métastabilité, Aubier, Paris 1989.

57 Simondon, *Du mode d'existence*, pp. 128–9. [Tr. note: translated from the Italian.]

58 Bruno Latour, *We Have Never Been Modern*, trans. Catherine Porter, Harvard University Press, Cambridge Massachusetts 1993, p. 142ff.

59 Ibid., p. 136. On this question, see G. Leghissa, "Ospiti di un mondo di cose. Per un rapporto postumano con la materialità," in *aut aut*, 361 (2014), pp. 10–33.

60 Jonathan Kingdon, *Self-Made Man and His Undoing*, Simon and Schuster, London 1993, p. 3.

61 See Gottard Günther, *Beiträge zur Grundlegung einer operationsfähigen Dialektik*, 2 vols., Meiner, Hamburg 1979.

62 Peter Sloterdijk, *Nicht gerettet. Versuche nach Heidegger*, Suhrkamp, Frankfurt am Main 2001. [Tr. note: there is no English translation of this work. Quotes are translated from the Italian] Italian edition: *Non siamo ancora stati salvati. Saggi dopo Heidegger*, Bompiani, Milano 2004. This quote p. 170. To read more about Sloterdijk and more generally about the relationship between technics and life, see Timothy Campbell, *Improper Life. Technology and Biopolitics from Heidegger to Agamben*, University of Minnesota Press, Minneapolis 2013; as well as A. Lucci, *Un'acrobatica del pensiero. La filosofia dell'esercizio di Peter Sloterdijk*, Aracne, Rome 2014, pp. 87ff.

63 Sloterdijk, *Non siamo ancora stati salvati*, p. 182.

64 Ibid., p. 184.

65 Jean-Jacques Rousseau, *The Social Contract, A Discourse*

on the Origin of Inequality, and A Discourse on Political Economy, trans. G. D. H. Cole, Digireads, Stilwell KS 2006, p. 8.

66 Michel Foucault, "The Dangerous Individual," in *Politics, Philosophy, Culture: Interviews and other Writings, 1977–1984*, Routledge, New York/London 1990, pp. 125–51. This quote p. 134.

67 Michel Foucault, "The Birth of Social Medicine," in *Power, Essential Works of Foucault, Vol. 3*, Penguin Books, London 2002, pp. 134–56. This quote p. 141.

68 Michel Foucault, *The History of Sexuality, Vol. 1*, trans. Robert Hurley, Vintage Books, Random House, New York 1990, pp. 89, 145.

69 Ibid., pp. 144–5.

70 This change in paradigm is effectively analyzed by M. Calise, *Il partito personale. I due corpi del leader*, Laterza, Rome–Bari 2010, pp. 109ff.

71 See Judith Butler, "'Nous, le peuple.' Réflexions sur la liberté de réunion," in *Qu'est-ce qu'un peuple?*, La Fabrique, Paris 2013. An Italian translation is also available: "Noi, il popolo. 'Riflessioni sulla libertà di riunione,'" in *Che cos'è un popolo?*, DeriveApprodi, Rome 2014, pp. 43–62.